April 24, 2012

Bro. Charlie,

As I went through my books
I found this volume that
struck me as something you
might value and use.

I give it to you firstly.
as a tool in winning and
discipling sinners to our
Saviour. Secondly. as a seed
of remembrance of our friend-
-ship and fellowship at
Gospel Light.

Sincerely your friend
and servant

Thomas

SEED FOR SERMONS

SEED FOR SERMONS

by

JEROME O. WILLIAMS

AUTHOR OF

The Gospel of Christ
Definite Decisions
Pastor's Record of Funerals
Pastor's Record of Weddings
Sermons in Outline

BROADMAN PRESS
NASHVILLE, TENNESSEE

This book is manufactured under wartime conditions in conformity with all Government regulations controlling the use of paper and other materials.

Printed in the United States of America
4000—6-45—3

THIS BOOK
IS
AFFECTIONATELY DEDICATED
TO
THE PREACHERS AND CHRISTIAN WORKERS
WHO HAVE NOT HAD THE PRIVILEGES OF COLLEGE
AND SEMINARY TRAINING
BUT
ARE PERFORMING A MIGHTY MINISTRY
FOR THE MASTER

CONTENTS

CONTENTS

CONTENTS

FOREWORD

About two years ago the Broadman Press published my little book, *Sermons in Outline*. The wide use of this book has created a demand and brought many requests for another book on the same order. *Seed for Sermons* is the result and reply.

The purpose of this book is to suggest subjects, texts of Scripture, and the logical unfolding of the texts for presenting scriptural and spiritual messages. It is the hope that suggestions will start a line of thought in the heart of busy pastors and other Christian workers, which will grow into vital, living, dynamic messages.

The outlines are brief, with no illustrations or poems printed, since these may be supplied from many sources. They are presented in simple language and logical order so that they can be easily memorized and followed.

Some of these outlines have appeared in recent years in present or briefer form in *The Quarterly Review*, published by the Sunday School Board of the Southern Baptist Convention.

These brief messages are sent out with an earnest prayer that the Lord may use them to bring many souls to Christ, to enrich many lives in Christ, and to inspire consecrated service for Christ.

JEROME O. WILLIAMS

Nashville, Tennessee

THE SPIRITUAL BATTLE

I have fought a good fight. 2 Timothy 4:7.

This is one of the last sentences written by the
great apostle Paul. He took a backward look before making a forward move for his eternal reward. Paul fought a battle and defeated the enemy.
He played a game and was victorious. He ran a
race and won the prize. He lived a life and was
most successful. Paul rejoiced in glorious victory.
Note the following things about the subject.

1. PAUL FOUGHT IN THE SPIRITUAL REALM

As all others, Paul began his life in the realm of
the physical. He knew only the material side of life
until he met the Lord Jesus Christ on the way to
Damascus. He was successful in the life he had
chosen. But when he met Christ and experienced
the glorious things of the spiritual realm, he was
willing to count all physical and social advantages
but loss and refuse, that he might win Christ and be
found in him. After he accepted Christ, his greatest desire was threefold: first, to know Christ; second, to live for him; third, to reach others for him.
He lived the rest of his glorious life for Christ in
the spiritual realm, for he could say, "For to me to
live is Christ" (Phil. 1:21). He could also say, "The
life which I now live in the flesh I live by the faith
of the Son of God" (Gal. 2:20). The good life will
be lived in the spiritual realm while one is in the
flesh.

2. Paul Fought with Spiritual Resources

This great apostle not only lived in the spiritual realm but he fought with spiritual weapons. He was led by the Holy Spirit in all of the movements of life. The Holy Spirit gave him power to move, to speak, to endure, to suffer, to win, and to be victorious. He lived by faith. He was inspired by a sacred love. He was enriched by abiding hope. He was encouraged by the presence and power of God. The Lord Jesus Christ dominated the life of Paul and forced him to his greatest effort and best service. The revelation of God's grace, goodness, and mercy to Paul enriched his life, message, and service. Because God saved him, called him, informed him, and trusted him with his message, Paul determined to be true in all things at all times. The good fight was made because of God, the Holy Spirit, the Lord Jesus Christ, and the eternal message of life, light, and love.

3. Paul Fought for the Spiritual Reign

When Paul knew good and God, he was anxious that God and good should reign in every realm of life. He would have the Lord reign in social, political, economic, professional, and business life. His desire for the reign of the Lord was beyond his local community and was extended to all people everywhere. This desire forced him on and on in earnest, anxious, and consecrated service on four extended missionary journeys, touching many cities of two continents and some islands of the sea. He said of Christ, "He must reign, till he hath put all enemies under his feet" (1 Cor. 15:25). God the source of all good must reign eventually.

4. PAUL WON THE SPIRITUAL REWARD

"Henceforth there is laid up for me a crown of righteousness, which the Lord, the righteous judge, shall give me at that day." His crown was not to be a wreath of laurel, wild olive, pine, or parsley, as was given to the victor in earthly contests, but a crown of righteousness as a proof of his noble character and faithful service. Paul assures us that this crown awaits all who love Christ and long for his appearing. The crown of life will be given to all who are faithful unto death.

Seek the spiritual realm and resources and spend your energies for the spiritual reign in the life of all people everywhere, and the Lord will give the eternal reward of righteousness.

BELIEVERS BELONG TO GOD

Therefore glorify God in your body, and in your spirit, which are God's. 1 Corinthians 6:20.

This verse declares the sacredness of life and the fact that believers belong to God. The body, mind, soul, and spirit are in the possession of God and we should so live and serve to seek to magnify him. In this verse we see the following facts:

1. BELIEVERS BELONG TO GOD BY ACT OF CREATION

"So God created man in his own image" (Gen. 1: 27). Man was made by a special creative act of God in the moral and spiritual likeness of the Creator. Man was made in the divine image. He lives, moves, and has his being in God. The Creator is the giver and the sustainer of life. God created male and female and blessed them and expected them to be fruitful and multiply and replenish the earth, to subdue it and have dominion over the fish of the sea, the fowls of the air, and the beasts of the field. Man has a mission and he should honor God by performing it. Man becomes a spiritual child of God only by grace through faith in Christ by way of the spiritual birth. By creation man is a creature of God and by faith he becomes a child of God.

2. BELIEVERS BELONG TO GOD BY RIGHT OF REDEMPTION

"Ye are bought with a price." The price of the purchase was the death of Christ on the cross. Christ gave himself in death that all who will believe in

him might have eternal life. The Christ has pur-
chased the believer. The believer is not his own;
he belongs to Christ. His personality—body, mind,
and soul—belongs to the Lord and should glorify
him in every act, thought, and word. The Lord desires to use his own for the progress of his kingdom.

3. BELIEVERS BELONG TO GOD BY VIRTUE OF OCCU-
   PATION

"Know ye not that your body is the temple of the
Holy Ghost which is in you, which ye have of God,
and ye are not your own?" The Holy Spirit desires
to abide in the body, mind, and soul of the Christian.
He will dwell in the body and sanctify it and animate
it for his glory. The Holy Spirit will live in the
body of the believer and guide in the mind and il-
luminate it, enrich the soul and sanctify it. The
dwelling place of the Holy Spirit must be kept clean
and sacred unto its high and holy purpose. What a
comfort the believer has! What peace and joy!

4. BELIEVERS BELONG TO GOD FOR SERVICE

Since God created the body and gives the soul
eternal life through Christ, and the Holy Spirit
dwells in the body as his temple, the believer should
glorify God in the body and in the spirit. This can
be done by sacred living and consecrated service. All
that the believer is and can become by the help of
the Lord should be consecrated and used for his
glory.

Glorify God as Creator. Magnify Christ as Saviour. Follow the Holy Spirit as Leader. Honor life
by living it with the Lord.

THE BUSINESS OF BELIEVERS

Go ye into all the world, and preach the gospel to every creature. Mark 16:15.

These are the words of the Christ after his victory over death and the grave. In these words Christ committed to believers the big business of preaching his gospel to the whole world. He was speaking to his disciples. Though these were the immediate messengers, the Commission is unto all believers down through the ages. In the text we find these facts:

1. THE PERSONS OF THIS MISSION

"Go ye." The words of Jesus giving this commission were to the eleven disciples. They had been chosen from various walks of life and had spent three years in the school of Jesus and had come to know him and to love him and to have some conception of his kingdom. They had got to the place where Christ could trust them to do a big task for him and his kingdom. On these messengers depended the start which the gospel of Christ would have.

2. THE PLACE OF THIS MISSION

"Into all the world." These messengers were to begin in Jerusalem and extend the message of Christ to an ever-widening circle until it should reach all the world. The message was to reach all the islands of the seas and the continents of the globe. All places on earth are included in this commission of the Christ.

[6]

3. THE PURPOSE OF THIS MISSION

"And preach the gospel." These messengers were to preach the gospel of the Lord Jesus Christ as the power of God unto salvation to all who would believe and accept it. This was to be the first, foremost, and fundamental business of the disciples of Jesus. They were to preach the gospel by voice, pen, life, and in every other possible way.

4. THE PEOPLE OF THIS MISSION

"To every creature." It is clearly the purpose of the Lord Jesus Christ to send the gospel to all the people of all the nations of all the earth. The gospel is to be preached to the people of all tongues, races, colors, and climates. The mission is all-inclusive. All men everywhere are to have an opportunity to hear it. This is the only hope of the world.

5. THE PROGRESS OF THIS MISSION

Even though the gospel has been preached to the people on every continent and on almost every island of the sea, it has not been presented so that men everywhere would accept Christ and Christianity. Believers in Christ now have an enormous task to be finished. The world is in turmoil. The population of the world is mingled, and possibly the best opportunity for proclaiming the gospel to all people of all nations is immediately before us. It is a task that deserves the greatest and best that can be done by all believers who love Christ.

Accepting this great commission from the great Christ, let us challenge the world to accept him and love him and serve him.

THE NEW BIRTH

Verily, verily, I say unto thee, Except a man be born again, he cannot see the kingdom of God. John 3:3.

The first fifteen verses of the third chapter of John's Gospel is the classic on the new or spiritual birth. It is the great passage in the New Testament on regeneration. There may be some things in the passage that are difficult to understand, but these four statements are clear and simple and correct.

1. THE NECESSITY OF THE NEW BIRTH IS EXPRESSED

"Except a man be born again, he cannot see the kingdom of God." In another verse it is recorded that Jesus said to Nicodemus, "Ye must be born again." The spiritual birth is as necessary for the spiritual life as the physical birth is for physical life. That which is spiritual must come from God, and no one can have the spiritual life without the new or spiritual birth. It is essential. It is necessary. Without the new birth one cannot even see the kingdom of God and certainly could not enter it. It is necessary for the soul to be born into the spiritual realm.

Those who trust in morality, reformation, education, culture, generosity, or works, as: reading the Bible, attending church, being baptized, observing the Lord's Supper, ministering to the poor, for their spiritual life disregard the words of Jesus.

2. THE NATURE OF THE NEW BIRTH IS EXPLAINED

"Except a man be born again." In the margin the word "again" is translated "from above." It is, then, the birth from God which gives a man spiritual life. The new birth is from above, from God, and gives spiritual life to the soul. The new birth is divine nature imparted from the Father and received by the human heart. "That which is born of the Spirit is spirit." Jesus insists here upon the spiritual nature of the new birth. This is indeed a heavenly thing, for the wind bloweth where it will and we may hear the sound thereof but cannot tell whence it cometh or whither it goeth, and the birth of the Spirit is like this. We accept the Word of Christ. By faith we know him and love him. We know we are children of God.

3. THE AUTHOR OF THE NEW BIRTH IS ANNOUNCED

Jesus said, "Verily, verily, I say unto thee." The Lord Jesus Christ is the giver of spiritual life. He said, "The Son of man is come to seek and to save that which was lost" (Luke 19:10). He also said, "I am come that they might have life" (John 10:10). We read, "He that believeth on the Son hath everlasting life" (John 3:36). We are saved by grace through faith in the Lord Jesus Christ. Christians are the workmanship of God, created in Christ Jesus. What Christ did on the cross and what the Holy Spirit does now in us and for him makes it possible for us to become children of God. He is the author of our salvation. He is the giver of eternal life. The new birth is possible because of Christ. Blessed Lord Jesus! Believe in him!

4. The Possibility of the New Birth Is Experienced

Nicodemus came to Jesus by night, probably because that was the best time to have a conversation with Jesus. Though it is not positively stated, it can be accurately assumed that this distinguished person experienced the new birth while talking with Jesus. Good proof that he was devoted to Christ is shown in that he was one of the two who took his body from the cross, prepared it for burial, and placed it in the new sepulcher (John 19:39-42). The testimony of the fact of the new birth is abundant day after day now and has been through the ages. All who trust Christ may have spiritual life through the new birth.

You must be born again. You can be born again. You will be born again if you will yield your heart to Christ.

BLESSINGS FOR BELIEVERS

For all things are yours. 1 Corinthians 3:21.

What a promise to believers! What blessings for believers! Believers belong to Christ and Christ belongs to God; and they are promised all things, whether the world, or life, or things present, or things to come. Blessings for believers are too numerous to be listed. It is good to think on these glorious blessings. Add others to the ones mentioned here and proclaim them to the sinful world.

1. BELIEVERS RECEIVE ETERNAL LIFE

"He that believeth on the Son hath everlasting life" (John 3:36). This is the greatest gift that can be received. It is greater than any blessing that can be given by friend, or mother, or father, or angels and is the very greatest that God has to offer. It can be received only by grace through faith in the Lord Jesus Christ. Believers are most happy in this gracious gift. This is the supreme blessing.

2. BELIEVERS RETAIN TEMPORAL BLESSINGS

"Seek ye first the kingdom of God, and his righteousness; and all these things shall be added unto you" (Matt. 6:33). Those who receive eternal life and place the kingdom of God first in their thoughts and actions are promised all necessary temporal blessings. The Lord knows that food and drink and clothing are essential to the temporal life, and he assures the believer of all that is necessary when the kingdom is placed first. Temporal blessings are minor. The kingdom of God is the major for all Christians. When we seek the kingdom first we are assured of all else. This is a superb blessing.

3. BELIEVERS REST IN DIVINE PROTECTION

"All things work together for good to them that love God, to them who are the called according to his purpose" (Rom. 8:28). In these days of diseases, distresses, difficulties, dangers, and tragic deaths, it is good to be assured of divine care. It is true that the ravages of earth may destroy the body, but none of these can harm the soul that is resting in the eternal love of God. And the same God who cares for life has all power to comfort in life. It is a great blessing to rest in divine protection.

4. BELIEVERS REJOICE IN DIVINE FELLOWSHIP

John, the apostle, wrote, "Truly our fellowship is with the Father, and with his Son Jesus Christ" (1 John 1:3). Fellowship with family and friends and followers of Christ is sweet beyond expression. Believers have the supreme joy of fellowship with the Father and the Lord Jesus Christ. Surely no joy could be greater, no fellowship could be sweeter. This blessing of the believer is sublime.

5. BELIEVERS REACH DIVINE SERVICE

The apostle Paul said, "We are labourers together with God" (1 Cor. 3:9). Whom the Lord saves and justifies, he also calls for some definite service. The sincere soul can find this God-given service and qualify himself for it. He then has the real joy of working with the Lord who has all wisdom and power to assure success. Believers may work with God in salvation of sinners, in support of the suffering, in comfort of the sorrowing, in strengthening the weak, and in proclaiming his message. Angels do not have this privilege. This blessing of the believer should crown the Christ.

These blessings and many others are all for those who believe in the Lord Jesus Christ, and for those who will believe. Receive them and rejoice in them.

THE CALL OF THE LORD

The Master is come, and calleth for thee. John 11:28.

Even though these are words of Martha to her sister Mary when the loving Christ arrived to bless them in their sorrow, they are words which have a message and a meaning to every Christian. This call of the Lord is repeated many times through the New Testament. We call attention to some of these.

1. IT IS A CALL TO MARVELOUS LIGHT

"That ye should shew forth the praises of him who hath called you out of darkness into his marvellous light" (1 Peter 2:9). The Lord calls to all men to forsake darkness and turn to the glorious light of Christ. He desires all to live in this light through their days on earth and then to enjoy the most glorious rays of the same light in the heavenly life to come, where there is no need of the sun, moon, or stars, for he is the Light of the place.

2. IT IS A CALL TO A GLORIOUS KINGDOM

"That ye would walk worthy of God, who hath called you unto his kingdom and glory" (1 Thess. 2:12). His kingdom is the realm in which his will is thoroughly understood and observed. To this happy realm he calls all who will believe on him and accept his will and follow in his way.

3. IT IS A CALL TO BLESSED FELLOWSHIP

"God is faithful, by whom ye were called unto the fellowship of his Son Jesus Christ our Lord" (1 Cor.

1:9). The most blessed fellowship possible in this life and in the life to come is fellowship with the Father, the Son, and the Spirit. "Truly our fellowship is with the Father, and with his Son Jesus Christ" (1 John 1:3). Fellowship with the Father makes fellowship with one another sweeter and stronger.

4. It Is a Call to Higher Heights

"I press toward the mark for the prize of the high calling of God in Christ Jesus" (Phil. 3:14). The apostle Paul is the example for all believers. He would admonish all now to forget the things which are behind and reach forth unto those things which are before and to press forward for the prize of the high calling of God in Christ Jesus. The highest heights that may be reached by any soul are those by the side of the Lord Jesus Christ.

5. It Is a Call to Holy Living

"For God hath not called us unto uncleanness, but unto holiness" (1 Thess. 4:7). He has called us with a holy call, not according to our works, but according to his purpose and grace which was given us in Christ Jesus. As he is holy, so he expects his followers to live the clean and holy life.

Thus we are called of the Lord to reach the marvelous heights and abide in blessed fellowship in the glorious kingdom on the heights with the Lord Jesus Christ.

THE PLACE CALLED CALVARY

And when they were come to the place, which is called Calvary, there they crucified him. Luke 23:33.

In every country there are many historical places. To every life there are many sacred places. In Palestine, just north of the city of Jerusalem, there is a place which is both sacred and historical. It is the place called Calvary. It is sacred because there the Christ, the Saviour of the world, was crucified for the sins of the world. It is historical because that event is the most important one in the religious life of the world.

We point out some of the important things that happened in this place called Calvary:

1. IT WAS A PLACE WHERE THE PERSON WAS CRUCIFIED

On this place called Calvary, the Skull, or Golgotha, the Lord Jesus Christ was crucified for the sins of the people of the earth. The greatest Person of all ages died for the greatest purpose for all people.

2. IT WAS A PLACE WHERE PEOPLE WERE ASSEMBLED

On the brow of Calvary great crowds were gathered to look upon the scenes surrounding the crucifixion of Christ. They were there from many nations: Jews, Greeks, Romans, Syrians, Assyrians, Egyptians, Babylonians, and others. They were there also from every walk of life: scribes, Pharisees, Sadducees, Sanhedrists, disciples, soldiers, and the common people. Multitudes were gathered on Calvary.

3. It Was a Place Where Prayer Was Offered

As the soldiers raised the cross on which the body of Jesus was nailed, Jesus cried, "Father, forgive them." This is a sincere prayer of the Saviour for all those who had anything to do with his crucifixion —Judas, Pilate, Herod, the chief priests, scribes, members of the Sanhedrin, the people, the centurion, and the soldiers. The Saviour prayed for forgiveness for the sins of every one of them.

4. It Was a Place Where Praise Was Proclaimed

When Christ was crucified Pilate wrote a superscription and placed it above the cross. This superscription was possibly "Jesus of Nazareth, King of the Jews." It was written in the Greek, Latin, and Hebrew languages. The Greek language is a symbol of culture, the Latin of power, and the Hebrew of piety. Pilate thus crowned the Christ as King in the realm of culture, power, and piety. The greatest praise was proclaimed by this deed of Pilate.

5. It Was a Place Where Protection Was Provided

As Jesus hung on the cross he saw his mother and the disciple whom he loved standing by, and he said to his mother, "Woman, behold thy son." He then spoke to the beloved disciple, "Behold thy mother." The heart of John understood, and from that moment he took the mother of Jesus into his own home

and cared for her with the tenderest affection.
Christ on the cross was interested in the protection
of his mother.

6. It Was a Place Where Pardon Was Completed

By the side of the cross on which Jesus was crucified there were two other crosses on which malefactors were crucified. As the three were dying one
of the malefactors called upon the Christ to help
him, and Jesus spoke to him saying, "Today shalt
thou be with me in Paradise." The pardoning power of the blood of Christ was tested even before one
drop had touched the earth. The plan for pardoning of sin was completed on Calvary.

7. It Was a Place Where Great Pain Was En-
dured

The agony of Christ on the cross is beyond the
feeling of the human heart. Often pain in the physical body is almost more than can be endured. Yet
the pain and agony of the mental and spiritual life
is more severe than that of the physical life. Jesus
knew the ruin of sin, the unspeakable destiny of the
soul in sin. The horror of it all hastened his death,
and in unspeakable agony he died on the cross on
the place called Calvary.

8. It Was a Place Where the Plan of Salvation
Was Perfected

Near the end of his hours on the cross he cried,
"It is finished." The life of the Son of God on earth
had come to an end; his suffering on the cross was
complete. The plan of salvation for every soul was

finished. The way from earth to heaven was finished. The way from the heart of man back to the heart of God had been completed. Christ who died on Calvary had completed the way for all men to be saved.

THE CHILD IN THE MIDST

Jesus called a little child unto him, and set him in the midst of them. Matthew 18:2.

When Jesus desired to teach his disciples some very important lessons, he called a little child and set him in the midst of them and said, "Become as little children." We call attention to some of the lessons to be learned from the child.

1. THE CHILD IS TRUSTFUL

The child places implicit trust in the words, will, and ways of mother. It believes in mother. It has faith in parents and lives by this faith. So must disciples of the Lord have implicit faith in him and trust him to supply every spiritual and material need of life, for all live and move and have their being in him. He is abundantly able and anxiously willing to supply every need. Trust the Lord.

2. THE CHILD IS DEPENDENT

The little child is helpless. It is dependent on mother or nurse or someone else for every need of life—as food, drink, clothing, and all other essentials. So are the children of God dependent on him for spiritual life, for every good and perfect gift comes from him. Spiritual needs cannot be supplied by any other being or from any other source. The disciple of the Lord is solely dependent on the Lord. Depend on the Lord. He will never fail you nor forsake you.

3. The Child Is Loving

As the child believes in mother and trusts her to supply every need, so does it love mother with all of its being. Fears are calmed when mother is near. Troubles cease in mother's arms. The little life loves mother with every devotion. So must disciples love the Lord and look to him for comfort and constant fellowship. Believers are to love the Lord with the whole heart, soul, mind, and body. The Lord Jesus is worthy of such loving devotion.

4. The Child Is Obedient

The child learns to obey the voice of mother. The loving child rejoices to anticipate the desire of mother and to do her will before she expresses it. So the disciple of Jesus must be obedient to every word and wish of his. He will rejoice to obey the word of Jesus and to walk in the way of Jesus and to perform the will of Jesus. Obedient disciples are happy disciples.

"Become as little children" and trust the Lord Jesus for every blessing of life, depend on him to supply every need of life, love him devotedly with every element of life, and serve him with every fiber of your being.

A NEW CREATURE IN CHRIST

If any man be in Christ, he is a new creature.
2 Corinthians 5:17.

The hope of the individual soul and of the world is to be found in new creatures in Christ. Human nature must be changed. The sinful nature and desire must be replaced by the spiritual nature. This change in human nature can come about only by the power of Christ through the work of the Holy Spirit in the individual heart. This we call regeneration or the new birth.

Regeneration is more than reformation or a loud profession, or culture, or morality, or good works, or church membership, or the act of baptism. It is more than a desire in the right direction. It is a complete change of the heart by the power of God. We note three characteristics of this change.

1. IT IS A DIVINE CHANGE

The Bible teaches that man is conceived and born in sin and iniquity (Psalm 51:5). It also teaches that God desires truth in the inner man. The change from a sinful heart to a heart of truth must be by divine power. Jesus said to Nicodemus, "Ye must be born from above" (John 3:7). If it was essential for him to be born from above, it is necessary for all. Those who would become sons of God are to be born "not of blood, nor of the will of the flesh, nor of the will of man, but of God" (John 1:13). The divine change is the spiritual birth, for "that which is born of the Spirit is spirit" (John 3:6).

Regeneration is the work of God in changing the human heart from its sinful state to a new creature in Christ.

2. IT IS A MYSTERIOUS CHANGE

Man may not be able to understand and explain this divine change, for it is mysterious, but he can accept it. Jesus said, "The wind bloweth where it listeth, and thou hearest the sound thereof, but canst not tell whence it cometh, and whither it goeth: so is every one that is born of the Spirit" (John 3:8). Electricity is mysterious. We cannot explain it. However, we accept it to give us light and power and to transmit messages. We cannot explain how food is taken into the body and masticated, digested, and assimilated into blood, bone, tissue, and all other elements of the body, but we continue to accept food. We may not be able to explain how an egg, which is composed of food elements for the body, when kept at a certain temperature for a stated time will hatch a little chick, but we accept both the egg and the chicken. Many mysteries meet us daily and we accept them. We may not be able to explain how the Lord saves us by grace through faith in Christ, but we can know it is a fact. We thank the Lord for new life in Christ and accept it and use it for his glory.

3. IT IS A UNIVERSAL CHANGE

"If any man be in Christ, he is a new creature: old things are passed away; behold, all things are become new." The old nature is full of "anger, wrath, malice, blasphemy, filthy communication out of the mouth" (Col. 3:8), but the new heart is holy and beloved and full of mercy, kindness, humbleness of mind, meekness, longsuffering, forgiveness, and charity, which is the hand of perfection. Regeneration is a complete and universal change. The person in Christ is a new creature. He has a new heart and a new conscience to govern it. He has a new purpose and a new will to perform it. He has a new song and a new voice to sing it. He has a new spiritual eye and new visions to behold. He has a new hope and a new faith to realize it. He sees a new home and has a new determination to reach it. He is a new creature and walks with a new Master. He is completely made over and is a new creation.

Thus the radical change from sinner to saint is mysteriously wrought in the human heart by the power of God by grace through faith in Christ, and the person becomes a new creature in Christ.

CHRIST LIFTED UP

So must the Son of man be lifted up. John 3:14;
8:28; 12:32.

God and man are both involved in this matter of
lifting up the Son of man. Man lifted him on the
tree but it was in fulfilment of the plan of God. God
lifted him out of the tomb and placed him on the
throne. Man must lift Christ up in testimony.

1. CHRIST WAS LIFTED UP ON THE TREE

It was essential that Christ should die on the
cross. The children of Israel had a lesson in faith
and obedience in the wilderness. When they spoke
against God and Moses, the Lord sent serpents to
bite them and cause many to die. When the people
saw their sin and the punishment, they cried to
Moses confessing their sin. The Lord told Moses to
put a brazen serpent on a pole and bid the people
bitten by the fiery serpent to look upon it and live.
It was so. Now as Moses lifted up the serpent in
the wilderness, so must the Son of man be lifted up.
The fact is, all men are sinners; and Christ has been
lifted up on the tree. Peter says of him, "Who his
own self bare our sins in his own body on the tree"
(1 Peter 2:24). Sinful man nailed Christ to the
cross, but "Christ died for our sins according to the
scriptures" (1 Cor. 15:3). Friend and foe testi-
fied to the death of Christ.

2. CHRIST WAS LIFTED OUT OF THE TOMB

When the body of Jesus was dead on the cross,
friends came to remove it and prepare it for burial

and to place it in the new tomb of Joseph. The tomb was hewn out of rock and when the body was placed in it a great stone was rolled against the door of the sepulcher. Later the Jewish rulers secured permission from Pilate to seal the tomb with the king's seal and to place soldiers to guard the tomb to see that the body was not taken away. But in the morning of the third day an angel of the Lord descended from heaven and rolled away the stone, and Christ came forth the living Lord and King of kings. "He was raised again for our justification" (Rom. 4:25). Christ was lifted out of the tomb by the eternal power of God. This same power God is willing to manifest for the good of people (Eph. 1:19).

3. CHRIST WAS LIFTED UP TO THE THRONE

After many appearances before his disciples and definite proof of his life and certain added teachings, the God of heaven lifted up the Christ "and set him at his right hand in the heavenly places" (Eph. 1:20). He ascended from the mount called Olivet as recorded in Acts 1:9-12. He was given a place most high above all things (Eph. 1:21-22). He was given a name which is above every name (Phil. 2:9-11). Christ was lifted up by the Father and given a place on the throne where he ever liveth to make intercession for sinners (Heb. 7:25).

4. CHRIST MUST BE LIFTED UP BY TESTIMONY

Believers in Christ must lift him up before the lost world as the only Saviour from sin. If he is lifted up he will draw men by his power, his grace, his love, his unselfish suffering, and will give unto them eternal life.

Lift him up. Hold him before the eyes of men. Let them see eternal life by grace through faith in Christ.

THE CHRIST OF GOD

Study the first three verses of chapter one in Hebrews and find the following eight wonderful facts about the Christ of God.

1. HE WAS THE SON OF GOD

"God . . . hath . . . spoken unto us by his *Son*." The voice of the Father verifies the fact more than one time that Christ is his Son. "This is my beloved Son" (Matt. 3:17). "This is my beloved Son: hear him" (Luke 9:35). The disciples came to realize this truth, and one declared "Thou art the Christ, the Son of the living God" (Matt. 16:16). Christ is the Son of God and therefore divine.

2. HE WAS THE SPOKESMAN FOR GOD

"God . . . hath in these last days *spoken unto us by his Son*." The Son of God came to earth as the voice of the Father, and he speaks for the Father and in the name of the Father to the people of the world in every age. He is God's spokesman and man receives God's message through him. Listen to his voice and learn his message.

3. HE WAS THE HEIR OF GOD

"Whom he hath appointed *heir of all things*." Christ being the Son of God has the right to inherit all of the attributes of the character of God. The elements of character in the Father such as holiness, righteousness, love, mercy, and grace were inherited by the Son and he manifested the same to the people of the earth. He is heir of all things. Believers may become joint heirs of God with Christ and thereby be enriched with all the glories of heaven and earth.

4. HE WAS CREATOR WITH GOD

"By whom also *he made the worlds.*" Christ the Son was with God the Father in the hour of creation. "All things were made by him; and without him was not any thing made that was made" (John 1:3). Christ was with the Father from the beginning and joined him in the creation of all things and continues with him and is therefore eternal.

5. HE WAS THE IMAGE OF GOD

"Who being the brightness of his glory, and the *express image of his person.*" Christ completely manifested the character and brightness and glory and image of God the Father on earth before men. While in the human body he was divine and exemplified divinity in all of his acts. He adequately expresses the image of God.

6. HE WAS THE SUSTAINER OF GOD

"Upholding all things *by the word* of his power." He was not only the image of God but he manifested and supported and upheld and magnified the character of God the Father in all contacts of life.

7. HE WAS SAVIOUR FOR GOD

"When he had by himself *purged our sins.*" "God so loved the world, that he gave his only begotten Son, that whosoever believeth in him should not perish" (John 3:16). The Father sent the Son into the world that through him the world might be saved. He is the one who makes satisfaction with God for the sins of the world. He is the Saviour.

8. HE WENT ON HIGH TO GOD

"Sat down on the right hand of *the Majesty on high*." When Christ had lived on earth and had given himself in death on the cross and had been buried by loving hands in the new tomb and had arisen from the dead by the power of God and manifested himself by infallible proof before men, he went back to the Father to make intercession for us. He is on the throne at the right hand of the Majesty on high.

This glorious Christ of our gracious God is the only hope of the world now and evermore.

CROWDS ABOUT CHRIST

And all the city was gathered together at the door.
Mark 1:33.

Mark gives us this picture of the multitudes seeking the Master. Jesus had spent the sabbath day in Capernaum teaching in the synagogue and healing in the home of Simon. "At even, when the sun did set" and the sabbath was ended, the multitudes gathered about the Lord. Note these phases of the event.

1. THE PEOPLE WERE NEEDY

The people who were brought to Jesus were sick of divers diseases and possessed of devils. They were unable to come to Jesus in their own strength. They were in dire need. Those who brought these to Jesus were citizens of the favored city of Capernaum and neighbors of Jesus. Thus, people of all classes and conditions came to seek the Saviour. Those who bring others to Jesus and those who are brought will receive the blessings of the Lord.

2. THE PLACE WAS CONVENIENT

It was in the city and thus near to the needy multitudes. It was at the door of the private home of Simon and Andrew. On the inside of the house was the Person who said, "I am the door" (John 10:9). Wherever Jesus is, is a good place for people to assemble. Wherever Jesus is presented as the living Christ and the Saviour from sin, people will gather in large numbers even in this day. This brings a grave responsibility on the pastor in the pulpit, the teachers in the classes of the Sunday school, and the directors of the training services. Lift up the Lord and lead the people to him.

3. THE PURPOSE WAS EVIDENT

It is evident that the sick desired to be healed and those possessed of devils desired to be set free, and those who brought these to the Master believed he had power to heal and cast out devils. These also felt that the Lord was willing to manifest this power. These are two great truths about the Lord Jesus Christ: he is both able and willing to bless all needy people who come to him in faith. Bring the needy people to Jesus. He will bless them. Blessed are those who desire to see Jesus, to hear Jesus, and to be blessed by Jesus.

4. THE POWER WAS MANIFESTED

"He healed many that were sick of divers diseases, and cast out many devils." Only the Christ could do this mighty work. He alone has this matchless power. He is always ready to use this power for the good of needy people when they come to him in faith. His power is unlimited and will be used. He said, "All power is given unto me in heaven and in earth." Let sinners seek the power of the Saviour and be saved from sin.

5. HIS POPULARITY WAS INCREASED

The good news of the great ministry of the Master spread quickly over the city. On the very next day others came to see and to hear and to be blessed by Jesus, and the disciples went to him in a solitary place of prayer and said to him, "All men seek for thee." Would that all men everywhere would in all sincerity seek the Lord Jesus Christ. He must increase. He will increase.

Bring needy men to the Master for his matchless blessings and seek to crown him as Lord of all.

THE CRUCIFIXION

There they crucified him.   Luke 23:33.

How full these words! What volumes are in them!
How important the event here recorded!   What
pathos here expressed!

Each word in this brief text has a message.   We
seek to point out some thoughts which each word
suggests.

1. THE PLACE OF THE CRUCIFIXION WAS CALVARY

"There they crucified him."   Think of all of the
most historic places on earth, where men were born
or died, treaties were signed, nations were born,
buildings were erected, agreements were made, and
you will come back to Calvary and say, "This is the
most historic place on earth."   Think of all the sacred places on earth, where marriage vows are said,
where children are born, where bodies are buried,
where the Lord saved, and you will come back to
Calvary and say, "This is the most sacred place on
earth."   Calvary is the place where Christ was crucified and died.   The place is sacred and historic because of the importance to the human race of what
happened there ages ago.

2. THE PEOPLE OF THE CRUCIFIXION WERE CRUEL

"There *they* crucified him."   Those who nailed
Jesus to the cross on Calvary were Jews and Romans.   The rulers of the Jews passed the death sentence.   The Jewish people cried again and again,

"Crucify him! Crucify him!" and followed him to Calvary and mocked him. Pilate, the Roman governor, delivered him unto the mob to be crucified (John 19:16). The Roman centurion gave the orders, and the Roman soldiers drove the nails into his flesh to fasten his body to the cross and raised the cross upright. The people who crucified Christ were cruel, but those who sin against him now are guilty of the same crime, for he was crucified for all sinners. Sinners crucify Christ.

3. THE PAIN OF THE CRUCIFIXION WAS CUTTING

"There they *crucified* him." Crucified Christ! They stripped his garments from his body, placed his body on the cross, and drove cruel nails in his hands and feet. The blistering Syrian sun ceased to shine at noonday by the will of the sympathizing Father. Nailed to the cross, the body of Christ bled and suffered agony, even the agony as if all men were dying at one time. It was more than physical agony. It was more than the pain of the body. It was more than mental agony. It was agony of soul. It was the suffering of the Son of God. Other men were crucified, but no other man could suffer as did Christ. In a remarkably short time Christ died on the cross. He gave up the ghost and commended his soul unto the Father.

4. THE PERSON OF THE CRUCIFIXION WAS CHRIST

"There they crucified *him*." He came from God to earth to reveal the character of God to man. He was the one Person who had lived on earth among men, without sin. He came to do the will of God and he did it perfectly, for he did always the things that pleased the Father. He was divine. He was the Son of God. They crucified Christ. Christ surrendered his will to the will of the Father and died on the cross of Calvary.

5. The Purpose of the Crucifixion

"There they crucified him." "Christ died for our sins according to the scriptures" (1 Cor. 15:3). "The blood of Jesus Christ his Son cleanseth us from all sin" (1 John 1:7). "Jesus Christ . . . is the propitiation for our sins: and not for ours only, but also for the sins of the whole world" (1 John 2:2). Christ made atonement for all sins of all men of all the earth. His death makes it possible for all men to be saved by grace through faith in him. No other death could mean so much for the people of the earth.

This brief text mentions the most sacred place, the most cruel people, the most painful death of the most important Person for the supreme purpose.

DESIRES OF DAVID

Shew me thy ways, O Lord; teach me thy paths.
Lead me in thy truth. Psalm 25:4-5.

These sentences express the deep desire of the soul of David. His desires are most worthy. He prayed to the Lord for help to realize the holy ambitions of his heart. Both his desire and his method to attain are most commendable.

1. DAVID PRAYED FOR VISION

"Shew me thy ways, O Lord." He prayed not only for a vision of a way but for wisdom to see the ways of the Lord. He had a desire to see the mercy, goodness, loving-kindness, justice, and righteousness of the Lord. He wanted to see how the Lord treats both sinner and saint. A vision of the Lord and of what he has done, is doing, and will do, and how he does it would greatly enrich the heart of any person. "Where there is no vision the people perish." Where there is a clear vision of the Lord and his plan, as Paul had, a soul can march forward to do great things for the Lord. Lord, give us a clear vision of thee and of thy plan.

2. DAVID PRAYED FOR KNOWLEDGE

"Teach me thy paths." The desire of David was for more than a mere vision of the Lord's ways. He wanted to know the paths of the Lord. He desired to experience in his own heart the grace of God— his mercy, goodness, justice, and righteousness. It seems to be an earnest prayer to God that these holy

[37]

characteristics might become real knowledge in his life. Men learn by experience. They come to know the grace of God when they confess sin, and the Lord forgives. They know the goodness of God by his unspeakable gifts of life, light, love, health, and happiness. It is good to know the Lord and his plan by personal experience of his presence and power. He has the way for every life. He will teach the one who is meek and has faith. This path of mercy and truth can be found by talking to him in earnest prayer. "Teach me thy paths."

3. DAVID PRAYED FOR GUIDANCE

"Lead me in thy truth." It seems that this prayer of David was for more than a vision of the Lord's way and a clear knowledge of his truth, for he desired to be led into the Lord's character, paths, and plans. He had a desire actually to be like the Lord in his mercy, goodness, kindness, and righteousness. It is one thing *to see* and another thing *to be*. It is good to see, better to know, but best to be and to do. When the Lord guides the meek and faithful in his way the end will be success.

Pray unto the Lord. Pray for vision, knowledge, and guidance, and then follow in the Lord's way to victory.

REQUIREMENTS OF DISCIPLES

Whosoever doth not bear his cross, and come after me, cannot be my disciple. Luke 14:27.

Christ needs true disciples. He calls them from those who believe in him. He makes certain requirements of those who would be true disciples. His standards can be attained. We mention four of these requirements:

1. DISCIPLES MUST BELIEVE IN CHRIST

He who would be a disciple of Christ must trust him as Saviour from the power, penalty, and punishment of sin. He must believe in the ministry and message of Christ. He must also recognize him as Lord of all in his life. He must put Christ first in his affections, devotions, and activities. The disciple of Christ must love Christ above parents, self, relatives, material things, pleasure, or anything else in life. The Lord will have first place in the devotion of the heart of a true disciple. He is Lord of all or not Lord at all. The disciple must believe in Christ.

2. DISCIPLES MUST LEARN OF CHRIST

A disciple is a learner. He will enter the school of Christ and learn of the Lord and from the Master Teacher. Jesus said to his disciples, "Learn of me." We may learn of him from the Bible for the Old Testament prepares for his coming, the Gospels record his earthly ministry, and the other books of the New Testament interpret his life and message.

We may learn of him by serving with him, suffering with him, and by fellowship with him and with his people. The disciple of Christ will seek to know his way, will, work, and wonders. The Holy Spirit will gladly guide us to this knowledge (John 14:26; 15:26).

3. DISCIPLES MUST SERVE FOR CHRIST

"Whosoever doth not bear his cross." This indicates that there is some assignment for every true disciple. Christ bore his cross. He suffered on the cross for all men. He became the atonement for believers. Now he expects those who would be his disciples to be cross-bearers. Each disciple must bear his cross for Christ. The Lord gives every believer the ability to perform some task for him. This special duty must be found and performed. Some burden may be upon a believer. If it is of the Lord, it must be borne for his glory. Duty may be difficult, but if it is of the Lord, he will give power to perform it. Disciples must serve for the glory of Christ.

4. DISCIPLES MUST FOLLOW AFTER CHRIST

"And come after me." The Lord Jesus Christ is the ideal example before all believers. He is the ideal in life and in service. He went about doing good. He went about his work wisely. He did always that which pleased the Father. He did that which would elevate man. He was always able to accomplish things for the glory of God. Disciples of Christ must follow the example of Christ. He is the Way of life, and love, and light. The true disciple will follow him.

Believe in Christ; learn of Christ; serve for Christ. Follow Christ and you will glorify the Christ.

THE FAITH OF A FATHER

Lord, I believe; help thou mine unbelief. Mark 9:24.

A study of this incident in the life of Jesus, as recorded in the Gospel of Mark (9:14-29), will reveal many things about the faith of the father of the boy. Among these are:

1. THE CONDITION WAS A CALL FOR FAITH

The distracted father brought his sadly afflicted son to the disciples for healing and they could not heal him. The boy was possessed by an evil spirit which seized him and dashed him down on the ground where he rolled, foaming and grinding his teeth, until his strength was exhausted. The evil spirit at times would cast the boy into fire and water to destroy him. The father was earnest and anxious about his son and was now embarrassed by the multitude and the failure of the disciples. It was a time which called for great faith.

2. THE CHRIST WAS A CHALLENGE TO FAITH

At the right moment, Christ appeared. He always does. The father related the story to Jesus and brought the boy to him and said, "If thou canst do any thing, have compassion on us, and help us." Jesus turns the man's words back on him, saying, "If thou canst?" As if to say, that is for you and not for me. It was not a question of the power and ability and willingness of Jesus, but it was a question of the father's faith. "All things are possible

[42]

to him that believeth." It is a challenge to faith to see what Christ will do in response to faith in him.

3. The Circumstances Brought a Confession of Faith

When Jesus challenged the father's faith he immediately made a confession of faith. He said, "Lord, I believe." It was to say, "I believe you are Lord and Master. I believe you can cast out evil spirits. I believe you can heal my son. I believe you are the only one who can heal him." Earnestly and sincerely the father confessed his faith in Christ. But he was willing to admit that his faith was possibly not sufficient.

4. The Crisis Brought a Cry for Faith

While the afflicted boy was down before Jesus and the disciples and the multitude as one dead, the father cried out and said with tears, "Lord, I believe; help thou mine unbelief." It was a cry for more faith. It was a cry for greater faith. It was a cry for strength for a weak faith. It was a plea for help that he might believe everything that was necessary for him to believe in order to attain the blessings of the Lord. The crisis will come in each life when more faith in Christ is needed.

5. The Conclusion Is a Conquest of Faith

Jesus commanded the dumb and deaf spirit to come out of the boy and leave him forever. The evil spirit made his last effort to destroy the boy and then left him as one dead. "But Jesus took him by the hand and lifted him up; and he arose." What a vic-

tory over evil in the name of Jesus! What a crown
of faith! A fitting climax of faith in Christ!

Have faith in Christ. Confess this faith. Increase this faith and use it for his glory.

OUR GREAT GOD

*God is our refuge and strength, a very present
help in trouble.* **Psalm 46:1.**

God is first in this text. He is first in all things.
He was first in creation, and should be given first
place and greatest honor in every life. The psalmist in this text points us to the one source of every
need of our soul.

1. GOD IS OUR SHELTER

"God is our refuge." When troubles overcome
us, and trials baffle us, and sorrows weigh us down,
and burdens are too heavy to bear, and dangers are
all about us, and doubt is in the soul, and difficulties
seem to be too great to be overcome, the Lord is our
refuge. He extends his loving arms, and in a gentle voice with pleading petition he invites us to come
to him for shelter. Take refuge in God from the
fierce storms of life. He will calm the soul and enrich the life.

2. GOD IS OUR STRENGTH

"God is our strength." Man is weak and wayward. He falters and fails and falls. Man will
doubt and push on into danger. Man is often helpless and heartless. There is no need for man to be
like this. The Lord has promised to be the strength
of the life of his people. God is our strength. He
has all the power we will need. He promises to use
this power for our good and his glory. We need
only to let the Lord be the strength of our life. He
longs for this privilege.

[45]

3. God Is Our Support

"God is a very present help in trouble." So often the soul of man comes to the place in life when the closest human being cannot help. It seems that strength must come from a source higher than man and from a power greater than man. When help of this kind is needed, the gracious God of this universe is willing and ready to help. He is very anxious to help in every temptation, every trial, and every trouble. Lean on the Lord and let him help. Call upon him and he will abundantly bless.

GOD'S THOUGHTS FOR ME

The Lord thinketh upon me. Psalm 40:17.

We are often concerned about what others think about us. It is more profitable, however, to know what the Lord thinks of us. We are assured in this text that the Lord does think upon us. In other passages of the Scripture we are told that his thoughts are accurate, numerous, constant, personal, helpful, and loving.

1. GOD'S THOUGHTS FOR ME ARE ACCURATE

"O Lord, thou hast searched me, and known me" (Psalm 139:1). This passage and many others bear out the statement that the Lord knows all about each one of us. He knows our down-sitting and our up-rising, our thoughts and desires and attitudes, and even the unspoken words of our tongue. He is thoroughly acquainted with all our ways.

2. GOD'S THOUGHTS FOR ME ARE NUMEROUS

"How precious also are thy thoughts unto me, O God! how great is the sum of them! If I should count them, they are more in number than the sand" (Psalm 139:17-18). This passage assures us that the Lord has many thoughts about each of us. His thoughts are numerous. They are more than the grains of sand that bar away the ocean waves. They are too numerous to be conceived of by human mind.

3. GOD'S THOUGHTS FOR ME ARE CONSTANT

"When I wake, I am still with thee" (Psalm 139:18). "Thou hast beset me behind and before, and laid thine hand upon me" (Psalm 139:5). "He hath said, I will never leave thee, nor forsake thee" (Heb. 13:5). "The Lord is on my side; I will not fear" (Psalm 118:6). These passages assure us over and over again that the Lord is all about us at all times and thinks of us constantly.

4. GOD'S THOUGHTS FOR ME ARE FOR HELPFULNESS

"The Lord will perfect that which concerneth me" (Psalm 138:8). "I will cry unto God most high; unto God that performeth all things for me" (Psalm 57:2). The accurate, numerous, and constant thoughts of the Lord are all for the purpose of helping us to reach the end and accomplish the purpose for which we are in life. He is our refuge and strength.

5. GOD'S THOUGHTS FOR ME ARE LOVING

"God commendeth his love toward us, in that, while we were yet sinners, Christ died for us" (Rom. 5:8). The mercy and love and grace of God for the human soul are expressed abundantly in his gift of his Son that we might have everlasting life. His love is superb and sublime.

My soul can rest in the precious thoughts of God the Father.

NUGGETS OF PURE GOLD

Pay thy debt, and live thou and thy children on the rest. 2 Kings 4:7.

These Old Testament stories are gold mines. They contain nuggets of pure gold for the spiritual life. We pick four of these nuggets out of this story recorded in the first seven verses of this fourth chapter of 2 Kings.

1. THE NUGGET OF NEED

"Thine handmaid hath not anything in the house save a pot of oil." The good husband had died leaving the widow and two sons, and the creditors took all the possessions of the family. When the prophet of God, Elisha, conferred with the family, the report was made that nothing was left on which to live. In relating her need to the prophet she was taking stock of the present and planning for the future. It is always good for any Christian to take stock of his spiritual standing before the Lord. This will reveal outstanding spiritual needs.

2. THE NUGGET OF EMPTY VESSELS

"Borrow thee vessels abroad of all thy neighbours, even empty vessels." The prophet was preparing the family for taking care of abundant supplies which would be granted by the Lord. It was essential therefore to have vessels empty, and clean. It is the same when a heart seeks abundant spiritual blessings. The heart must be emptied of all earthly desires and temporal longings and be ready to be filled with spiritual and eternal blessings. Such hearts the Lord can bless and fill with his grace and goodness.

3. THE NUGGET OF USE

"Thou shall set aside that which is full." The prophet instructed the poor widow to take the empty vessels and the single pot of oil which she had, and pour oil out of this pot and fill the vessels as the sons would bring them. Soon all the vessels available were filled. The lesson of use comes from this message. The Lord expects us to use what we have for his glory. We may not have much, but what we do have belongs to him and should be used in his service. Christians should use their time, talents, possessions, personality, and everything they have and can acquire for the glory of the Lord. It is a law of nature that use increases value and efficiency. Plant a grain of corn and reap a thousandfold. Cultivate a voice and sing his praises more sweetly. The mere use of a thing ordinarily increases its value and efficiency.

4. THE NUGGET OF LIVING

"Go, sell the oil, pay thy debt, and live thou and thy children on the rest." By using the single pot of oil the supply became abundant, even sufficient for paying all debts and supplying every need of the family. The Lord Jesus Christ on the cross has paid the debt for our sin and now he gives abundant grace for abundant living and abounding service to all who will accept and use his bounteous blessings. Life is living the abundant life.

As the soul estimates its need and stands before the Lord, ready and willing to receive and then to use what the Lord gives, so the life will be rich and abundant.

THE GOSPEL FOR THE POOR

The poor have the gospel preached to them.
Matthew 11:5.

Jesus used the words of this text to assure John the Baptist that truly the Christ was at hand. Since in the same sentence he refers to the blind, the lame, the leper, and the deaf, we think he means those who are poor in the goods of the world as well as the poor in spirit. From this text and the teaching of Jesus in the Gospels we learn the kind of gospel which is sufficient for the poor.

1. IT IS A SIMPLE GOSPEL

The gospel for the poor is a simple message. It can be stated in simple words so that the unlearned may understand it. The Holy Spirit can take the simple message and make it clear to the uneducated mind and the means of eternal life for those who are not trained. This is the glory of the gospel. It is life for all. Though it is profound and eternal truth, it can be appreciated and appropriated by the most unlearned. The glory of the simple gospel is that it can be adapted to meet the need of any and every heart. It has a way of inspiring those who accept it to do and be their best in every way. It is a glorious gospel.

2. IT IS A SYMPATHETIC GOSPEL

This simple gospel message which can be understood and appropriated by all has a deep and abiding sympathy for all. When it is declared to the lowly,

they can love it and appreciate it. It gives sight to
the blind, hearing to the deaf, health to the ill, hope
to the hopeless, joy to the sorrowing, victory to the
defeated, triumph to the troubled, and life to the
dead. It is a gospel with power to reach down to
the lowest and to lift him to the highness of a saint.
This gospel reaches out to all and for all and seeks
to love and lift. It is a sympathetic gospel.

3. IT IS A SERENE GOSPEL

It was clear when Jesus stated it. It was bright
from the lips of Jesus. It is shining truth when declared by a loving believer in Christ. It can be seen
by anyone who opens the spiritual eye. It can be
heard by the ear that will listen. It can be appropriated by the heart that will seek. It is a free gospel and can be obtained by the needy heart, without
money and without price. The most precious gift
of all life is eternal salvation that comes from the
acceptance of the gospel of Christ.

4. IT IS A SATISFYING GOSPEL

The testimony comes from people of all ages that
the gospel of Christ satisfies. The same testimony
comes from people of all nations of all the earth. It
satisfies people of all stations of life and all stages
of development. The gospel of Christ gives peace
and satisfaction to all souls that will accept it. It
forms the basis for character that will please the
Father.

Learn the simple gospel. Love it devotedly. De-
clare it faithfully. Live it accurately. Proclaim
it correctly.

HELPING OTHERS TO FAITH

How shall they believe in him of whom they have not heard? Romans 10:14.

The greatest service before Christians today is to get all people everywhere to believe in the Christ as the Saviour of the soul and the Lord of life. How can this be done? What can Christians do to help others to faith in Christ? These suggestions may help. Seek to get all unbelievers to:

1. LOOK UNTO THE LORD

"Looking unto Jesus the author and finisher of our faith" (Heb. 12:2). Jesus came to earth to reveal to men the character of God and to perfect the way of salvation for all who will accept him by faith. The story of the earthly life of Jesus was written by John that men might believe that Jesus is the Christ, the Son of God, and that believing they might have eternal life through his name (John 20:31). Those who have seen Jesus in the flesh or by faith have seen the Father (John 14:9). To know the true God and Jesus Christ is eternal life (John 17:3). Point sinners to the Lord Jesus Christ. Show him to them. Get sinful people to look on the Lord for he is the author of faith. It is useless to look to anyone else for salvation from sin.

2. LISTEN TO THE WORD

"Faith cometh by hearing, and hearing by the word of God" (Rom. 10:17). In no uncertain sounds, proclaim the Word of God to the sinful people of the world, simply and positively. The sinner may be persuaded to hear the Word of God as he quietly reads it from the pages of the Bible, or as it is read at the family altar, or as it is preached from the pulpit, or as it is quietly quoted in a personal testimony face to face. Preach the Word. Teach the Word. Proclaim the message of the Lord to sinful people. Speak it so it can be heard and understood and it will bring faith and eternal life to those who believe.

3. YIELD TO THE SPIRIT

"When he is come, he will reprove the world of sin, and of righteousness, and of judgment" (John 16:8). Jesus said, "When the Comforter is come . . . he shall testify of me" (John 15:26). Jesus said, also, "When he, the Spirit of truth, is come, he will guide you into all truth" (John 16:13). Lead the sinner into the presence of the Holy Spirit and depend on him to convict of sin, to testify of Christ, and to guide into truth and sinners will have faith in Christ and receive eternal life.

It is the business of Christians to present the Lord Jesus Christ, the author of faith, proclaim the Word of God positively, and to depend on the Holy Spirit to convict and save the sinner by grace through faith in Christ. May Christians have faith and be faithful and lead others to faith.

THE DIVINE INVITATION

Let him that heareth say, Come. Revelation 22:17.

All through the Bible the Lord extends the invitation to people to come to him for grace and goodness, mercy and meekness, health and happiness, power and peace, life and light, salvation and service. The gracious invitation is repeated here in the last chapter of the Bible.

1. HEAR THE INVITATION

"Let him that heareth." The Lord speaks the invitation. He proclaims it in many ways and in many places. The invitation is given earnestly and distinctly to individuals and to multitudes. Men should listen to the word of the Lord. They should hear the voice of the Lord. They should assume the attitude of Samuel when he said, "Speak; for thy servant heareth" (1 Sam. 3:10). And the attitude of Joshua when he said, "What saith my Lord unto his servant?" (Joshua 5:14) ; or Saul when he said, "Lord, what wilt thou have me to do?" (Acts 9:6). Listen to the Lord. Hear his invitation.

2. UNDERSTAND THE INVITATION

"The Spirit and the bride say, Come." When the invitation of the Lord is heard it must be understood. The invitation is to all men everywhere. It invites all to come to love, light, and life. It is universal and unlimited. God the Father, Christ the Son, and the Holy Spirit join in giving the invitation and offer all the riches of heaven and earth for time and eternity to all who will accept it and respond to it. Understand the source of the invitation and the purpose of it and the fulness of life that will come to those who respond to it. Know the earnestness with which it is given and the ability of the giver to bless abundantly.

3. EXTEND THE INVITATION

"Let him that heareth say, Come." When we hear the invitation of the Lord and understand it and respond to it, duty is upon us to extend it to others. We may extend the invitation by word of mouth, by manner of life, and by the written word. We can extend the invitation anxiously, enthusiastically, positively, sincerely, and continuously. The Lord will help those who engage in this work for reaching lost people and enlarging the kingdom. It is his will, way, and work and he graciously gives his servants a part in it.

Hear the invitation of the Lord. Understand all that is involved in it. Eagerly extend the invitation of the Lord to a waiting world.

THE ABUNDANT LIFE

I am come that they might have life, and that they might have it more abundantly. John 10:10.

This wonderful text presents Christ as the speaker, the source, and the sustainer of the abundant life. In fact the abundant life is possible only in and through the Lord Jesus Christ.

1. Christ Is the Speaker of the Abundant Life

"I am come that they might have life." The Scriptures give many reasons for Christ's coming into the world. Some of these may be mentioned.

Christ came into the world to reveal the character of God to men. He was deity in the flesh and revealed the goodness, grace, love, mercy, justice, holiness, and righteousness of God to man.

Christ came to be the mediator between God and man. "There is one God, and one mediator between God and men, the man Christ Jesus; who gave himself a ransom for all" (1 Tim. 2:5-6).

Christ came to call sinners to repentance. In the record he says, "I came not to call the righteous, but sinners to repentance" (Mark 2:17). His call to sinners is clear. No one could mistake his words.

Christ came to save sinners. Paul declares, "This is a faithful saying, and worthy of all acceptation, that Christ Jesus came into the world to save sinners" (1 Tim. 1:15). He came to save sinners. He is able and willing and ready to save all who will turn from sin by repentance and to him by faith.

[58]

Christ speaks of the abundant life. He speaks with authority. He speaks for the Father.

2. CHRIST IS THE SOURCE OF THE ABUNDANT LIFE

Christ says, "I am the life." He also says, "I am come that they might have life, and that they might have it more abundantly."

All life comes from the same source. The triune God is the giver of all life whether it be life of plants of the earth, or fowls of the air, animals of the forest, or fish of the sea.

Man might take a seed into the laboratory and analyze it into its component parts, and then take the same amount of these parts and make another seed. In every way but one it might be a perfect seed. The seed made by man would not have life in it. Life comes from God. Christ is God. Therefore Christ is the giver of life.

Spiritual life, the abundant life, comes from Christ. Reading the Bible, singing songs, worshiping in the church may be means of cultivating and developing spiritual life, but the life itself must come to the soul of man through Christ.

Christ is the giver of life. He is the only source of the abundant life. Look to him and live. Live in him and live abundantly.

3. CHRIST IS THE SUSTAINER OF THE ABUNDANT LIFE

We live and move and have our being in him. Every good gift and every perfect gift comes to us from the Father through Christ.

Christ says, "I am that bread of life" (John 6:48). As the physical life is sustained by physical bread, so is the spiritual life sustained by Christ. No one can constantly live the abundant life without Christ.

Christ is the water of life. As no physical body can live without water, so no spiritual life can live without Christ. He says, "The water that I shall give him shall be in him a well of water springing up into everlasting life" (John 4:14).

The abundant life must draw constantly from the Christ. He sustains life under all circumstances. He can make life the abundant life.

As the Lord Jesus Christ speaks of life, he is also the source of life and the sustainer of life. Look unto him and live.

ETERNAL LIFE

I give unto them eternal life; and they shall never perish. John 10:28.

Eternal life is the greatest blessing that heaven or earth can give to man. It is a blessing greater than can be given by parents, or friends, or saints, or angels and the greatest that God the Father has to offer. Only God can give eternal life. It must come by grace through faith in the Lord Jesus Christ. Note some reasons why it is eternal life.

1. IT IS BROUGHT BY AN ETERNAL PERSON

"I give unto them eternal life." These are the words of the Lord Jesus Christ. He is eternal. He was with the Father when the worlds were made, for we read "All things were made by him" (John 1:3). Also, "By his Son, whom he hath appointed heir of all things, by whom also he made the worlds" (Heb. 1:2). Christ, the giver of eternal life, is eternal for we read, "Jesus Christ the same yesterday, and today, and forever" (Heb. 13:8). Only an eternal person can give everlasting life.

2. IT IS BASED ON ETERNAL PASSION

"God so loved the world, that he gave his only begotten Son" (John 3:16). "God commendeth his love toward us, in that, while we were yet sinners, Christ died for us" (Rom. 5:8). The cross of Christ is evidence of the eternal love of God the Father and of Christ the Saviour for sinful man. Why should God love us so? How could his love be so great and eternal? Only such passion could provide eternal life for the soul of man. Eternal passion provides eternal life.

3. It Is Bequeathed by Eternal Promises

Over and over again and again we read the precious promises of God to give eternal life to the person who will believe on Christ. "They shall never perish." "He that believeth on the Son hath everlasting life" (John 3:36). "He that heareth my word, and believeth on him that sent me, hath everlasting life" (John 5:24). "This is the will of him that sent me, that every one which seeth the Son, and believeth on him, may have everlasting life" (John 6:40). God said it and I believe it. Trust Christ and be saved for time and eternity. With a hand and heart of faith reach for Christ and eternal life.

4. It Is Backed Up by Eternal Power

The promises of God must be true for they are made by the eternal power which is alone in him. "He is able also to save them to the uttermost that come unto God by him" (Heb. 7:25). The power of God which promises eternal life to the believer is the same power that created the universe, that saved the few from the flood, that stopped the sun at the prayer of a saint, that protected the Hebrew children in the fiery furnace and Daniel in the lions' den, that changed the life of Saul and raised Jesus from the dead. This eternal power assures eternal life to all who will trust Christ.

Receive eternal life as the free gift of God by grace through faith in Christ and rejoice in all time and eternity.

THE LIFT OF LOVE

Love never fails. 1 Corinthians 13:8 (Montgomery).

True love is of God, for God is love. Love in its highest reach is true affection and faithful devotion of the soul toward God and man. Love is an eternal boon to life. Note the lift of love in three brief statements.

1. LOVE ENRICHES LIFE

Life is greatly enriched when it goes out in true affection for man and faithful devotion toward God. Love will make all relations of life sweeter, all duties of life more delightful, all burdens of life more bearable, and all plans of life more pleasant. Love will enrich thought, desires, purposes, conversation, and activities of life. Love for God will make prayer and fellowship more real. Love for man will make service for humanity more sincere and pleasant. The life of love can be rich and full.

2. LOVE ENABLES LIFE

When life is dominated by true love inspired of God, it will grow and develop and serve for love "beareth all things, believeth all things, hopeth all things, endureth all things." Love enables parents to make the home happy. Love enables children to grow in body, mind, soul. Love enables the church to teach the Word, to win the lost, to worship the Lord, to minister to the needy, and to accomplish God's will on earth. Love will enable nations to live together on earth in peace and mutual helpfulness.

Love is the golden cord that binds man to man and all to God. Love enables.

3. LOVE ENDURES. "LOVE NEVER FAILS."

Other things may fail, but not love. It never fails. Prophecies shall fail and tongues shall cease and knowledge shall vanish away, but love shall continue. Love is eternal. Its effects are eternal. Its influence is everlasting. Love can take a human life and make it a saint. Love can extend the service of human hands through ages. True love will go on and on loving and serving unto the perfect day.

Magnify love. Experience love for God. Express love for all men. Be an example of a loving soul in a world of war. Try the way of love in all contacts of life.

MARY AT THE FEET OF JESUS

Mary, which also sat at Jesus' feet, and heard his word. Luke 10:39.

The Gospels give an account of three occasions when Mary, the sister of Martha and Lazarus, was at the feet of Jesus. Each time was for a different purpose and each occasion has a profound lesson for those who believe in Jesus. Read the record and learn the lessons.

1. MARY LEARNS AT THE FEET OF JESUS

"Mary, which also sat at Jesus' feet, and heard his word" (Luke 10:39). The home of Mary and Martha and Lazarus at Bethany seems to have been open at all times to Jesus, and he often resorted there for rest and comfort and sympathy. On this occasion Martha was cumbered about much serving while Mary sat at the feet of Jesus and heard his word. Jesus rebuked Martha and commended Mary saying, "One thing is needful: and Mary hath chosen that good part, which shall not be taken away from her." She sat at the feet of the greatest Teacher to learn of his loving heart, cheerful character, deep desire, worthy way, and eternal purpose. Mary had the right desire and went to get knowledge directly from the Lord. Hers was a blessed privilege. All who have faith in Jesus may learn from him lessons of eternal value.

2. MARY WEEPS AT THE FEET OF JESUS

"When Mary was come where Jesus was, and saw him, she fell down at his feet, saying unto him, Lord, if thou hadst been here, my brother had not died" (John 11:32). When loved ones are sick we are comforted by those who love us. When the sorrow of death comes, only the Lord Jesus Christ can speak peace to the soul. Lazarus died while Jesus was away. When Jesus came, Mary could go to him with a sorrowful soul and come away with a happy heart. Jesus understood and extended sympathy and gave comfort. "Cast thy burden upon the Lord, and he shall sustain thee" (Psalm 55:22). The Lord can help needy souls. He will never fail the trusting heart. The Lord will lift with abiding love.

3. MARY SERVED AT THE FEET OF JESUS

"Then took Mary a pound of ointment of spikenard, very costly, and anointed the feet of Jesus" (John 12:3). It was at the feast at the house of Simon in Bethany, and Martha served, and Mary wiped the feet of Jesus with her hair and anointed his body for burial. Jesus commended the understanding heart and beautiful deed of Mary in most complimentary terms. As long as the world stands this beautiful deed for Jesus will be spoken of as a memorial to Mary. Eternal service can be rendered for Jesus by those who love him and who will be led by his Spirit.

Learn of Jesus for such knowledge is of eternal value. Take sorrow to Jesus for he will never fail you. Serve Jesus for rich rewards will be given by him.

THE MESSAGE OF THE ANGEL

And the angel said unto them, Fear not: for, be-hold, I bring you good tidings of great joy, which shall be to all people. Luke 2:10.

This message of the angel is one of superlatives. It declares the greatest day in history, the greatest gift of all ages, the happiest relationship of all life, and the only hope for all the world. These phases of the subject we note briefly.

1. THE ANGEL DECLARED THE GREATEST DAY IN ALL HISTORY

"This day in the city of David." Many great days are mentioned in both ancient and modern history. Such was the day in ancient history when the Lord completed creation and called everything good (Gen. 1:31); called Abraham out of Ur of Chaldees (Gen. 12:4); called the children of Israel out of Egypt (Ex. 13:17-18). Other great days in modern history have reference to the time when treaties were signed, continents discovered, inventions perfected, and scientific discoveries made. But of all great days, the greatest was the day on which Christ was born. From the early ages the people had been looking forward to this day. Since that day all civilization has looked back to it and recognized it in all letters, treaties, and agreements of every nature. The birth of Christ marks the central point of time. It is the day when God came to earth in human flesh to reveal himself to men. It is the greatest day in all history.

2. The Angel Declared the Greatest Gift of All Ages

"A Saviour, which is Christ the Lord." The Bible records great gifts which have been given by individuals to others or to the cause of the Lord. Such gifts are those which Jacob gave to his brother Esau (Gen. 32) ; that which Solomon gave to the dedication of the Temple (2 Chron. 7:5) ; those which the queen of Sheba gave to Solomon (2 Chron. 9:9) ; those which the Wise Men brought to Jesus when he was born (Matt. 2:11) ; that which the widow placed in the offering on the altar in the Temple (Mark 12:44) ; and many others mentioned in the Book. The records reveal sacrificial gifts in modern times. Women have been known to take jewels from their bodies and place them on the altar for the Lord. A born cripple has been known to hobble to the front of the church and place his crutch on the altar to be sold and used for the work of the Lord. These are great and altogether worthy gifts but the greatest of all gifts was the gift of God on the day when he gave his only begotten Son that all who believed in him should not perish but have everlasting life. This is the supreme gift of all ages.

3. The Angel Declared the Happiest Relationship of All Life

"I bring you good tidings of great joy." The coming of Christ into the world made it possible for the individual soul to have direct personal relationship through him to God the Father. There are many very happy relationships in life; that of a happy married couple is sacred and sublime; that of parents with children is superb; that of friend to friend is an abiding joy; that of business and professional men with their fellows is a great joy. But the happiest of all relationships of this life is the relationship to God the Father through the Lord Jesus Christ. In him we have peace, joy, and satisfaction, superb and sublime. The angel declared the happiest relationship of life on earth and in heaven in time and in eternity.

4. THE ANGEL DECLARED THE ONLY HOPE FOR ALL THE WORLD

"Shall be to all people." Many things that happen in the world affect a large portion of the population of the earth, such as, the discovery of electricity; invention, development, and use of communication systems, as the telephone, telegraph, and radio; the development of means of transportation; scientific discoveries in the medical field, and others of similar significance. But the one event in the history of the human race which has affected and does affect the largest number of people is the coming of Christ into the world, as announced by the angel. He announced a Saviour for all people. All the people of all the nations of all the earth have found him sufficient when he is tested.

Thus the voice of the angel declared the greatest day of all history, the greatest gift of all the ages, the happiest relationship of all life, and the only hope for the people of all the world.

THE MISSION OF MAN

Lord, what wilt thou have me to do? Acts 9:6.

This question was asked by Saul of Tarsus when he met the Lord Jesus on the way to Damascus. The question intimates at once that when the Lord saves a person it is for a purpose. Saved men have a mission to perform for the Lord. This mission is certain and it may be found, accepted, and performed for the Lord.

1. MAN'S MISSION IS ACTUAL

Our Father is a God of purpose. He has a purpose in all of his acts. All creatures and creations of the earth have a purpose. All grains, fruits, and vegetables of earth are for a purpose and each one is true to its mission. The grain of wheat produces wheat. The peach tree bears peaches. So it is with all nature. It naturally follows that when God saves a person he saves him for a purpose. Whom the Lord saves he calls for a certain task or many tasks. Some talent or ability is given to each redeemed person. Every Christian has some mission or ministry to perform for the glory of God and the good of man.

2. MAN'S MISSION MAY BE ASCERTAINED

When the Lord assigns a mission to a person, he will help that person to find and perform it. One's mission may be determined by his tendencies, characteristics, position, or circumstances. These will partially determine what a person can and should do. The best way for a Christian to find God's mission

for him in life is to go directly to the Lord in earnest
and anxious prayer, and then listen to the voice of
the Lord and follow his leadership. The Lord's will
for Saul was pointed out to him by another Christian. The Lord will reveal his will to sincere seekers.
Find his will for work in life.

3. MAN'S MISSION SHOULD BE ACCEPTED

When the Christian goes to the Lord in prayer
seeking his will for life's service and the answer is
given clearly, the will and the work and the way of
the Lord should be accepted. One should then set
himself to prepare himself well to do perfectly the
work which the Lord has assigned. He should say,
"This is the task the Lord has assigned to me. I will
accept it and get ready to do it. It is my work for
the Lord. I will do it for his glory."

4. MAN'S MISSION MAY BE ACCOMPLISHED

The Lord will not impose an impossible mission
on a Christian. When a work is assigned the Lord
will give strength to accomplish it. "For we are labourers together with God" (1 Cor. 3:9). He will
never leave us nor forsake us. And he has all power
and will use it to accomplish his high and holy will
through earnest Christians. It is said of the early
disciples of Jesus: "They went forth, and preached
every where, the Lord working with them, and con-
firming the word with signs following" (Mark 16:
20). The Lord will bless Christians in his service.

Every Christian has ability to perform some service for the Lord. Find the task, accept it, prepare
for it, and do it for the glory of God and the progress of his kingdom.

NEAR THE KINGDOM, BUT LOST

Thou art not far from the kingdom of God. Mark
12:34.

Jesus had been on a tour of the country teaching,
preaching, and healing, and when he returned to
Jerusalem various classes of people came to him
with questions. The priests and elders came with
a question about his authority and he answered
wisely. The Pharisees and Herodians had a question about tribute to Caesar and he answered them
(Mark 12:17). The Sadducees asked him a question
about the resurrection and he answered them. Then
a lawyer came with a question. It is this man about
whom we speak now.

1. THE MAN WAS INTERESTED IN THIS MANNER OF LIFE

"Master, what shall I do to inherit eternal life?"
(Luke 10:25). This man had no doubt heard the
other questions and answers. He now tempted Jesus
with his question. It is fair to assume that the man
was really interested in eternal life for himself and
possibly for others. It is a question for all men to
ask and seek an answer to. It is the most important
question anyone could ask in sincerity. The soul's
response to the answer will determine the destiny of
the soul.

2. THIS MAN WAS INFORMED ABOUT THE MEANING OF THE LAW

"Thou hast answered right" (Luke 10:28). Jesus
answered the man by asking him, "What is written

in the law?" The man then read the law correctly (Luke 10:27), and Jesus commended him for it. One may have an intellectual knowledge of the grace of God and believe in it with his mind without accepting it and appropriating the rich blessings of it in his heart. This man was well informed about the law. He knew the meaning of it and could read it correctly and explain it. This is clear from the record in Mark 12:32-33. He was in his position because of this fact. Simply to know of the love of God is not sufficient for salvation.

3. THIS MAN WAS INCLUDED IN THE MESSAGE OF THE LORD

"This do, and thou shalt live," said Jesus to the man (Luke 10:28). All men are included in the love of the Lord and in his plan of salvation. Jesus pointed out this fact to this lawyer and pressed him to answer. However, the individual soul must respond to the love of God and accept it before he can claim the life which is available in it. He who loves the Lord supremely will accept eternal life from the Lord and honor him in devotion. Supreme love for the Lord will then answer every question of devotion, for if a person loves the Lord supremely he will attend church for Bible study, worship, prayer, and will support the cause of the Lord with life and means.

4. THE MAN WAS INVITED TO MAGNIFY THE LORD

"This do," Jesus said to the man. The man was invited to love the Lord supremely. He was admonished to magnify the Lord and his work. But as

Jesus mentioned love for neighbor the man sought to justify himself that he could not be sure who his neighbor was. Jesus gave an example and when he had pointed to the neighbor as the one in need, and how he was served by one who cared, he said to the man, "Go, and do thou likewise." Lives may magnify the Lord by loving him supremely and by loving and helping those who are in need.

5. THE MAN WAS INDIFFERENT TO THE MEASURE OF LOVE

Though this man was interested in eternal life and was familiar with the law and love of the Lord and answered Jesus discreetly, there is no record that he accepted the Lord Jesus Christ and eternal life through him. He heard the words but would not accept. He knew the way of life but would not walk in it. He knew about the light of God but would not live in it. He knew about the love of God but would not respond to it. He was at the door but would not enter. He was near the kingdom. Alas! to be near is not sufficient. "Almost persuaded" is not enough. A decision for Christ and life must be made. So far as the record goes, the man went away from the kingdom. Will you also go away?

This may be the story of many lives brought near the kingdom by a song, a sermon, a sorrow, a suffering or a saint. While you are near, enter. Go all the way.

PAUL'S HEAVENLY VISION

I was not disobedient unto the heavenly vision.
Acts 26:19.

The words of this text were spoken by the apostle
Paul to King Agrippa. They refer to his vision of
Christ on the way to Damascus and to his conver-
sion, and to his call and commission by Christ. The
following things were inspired in Paul and are inspired in others now by such visions.

1. SUCH HEAVENLY VISION SAVES THE SOUL

As Paul journeyed to Damascus the light from
heaven, brighter than the Syrian sun, fell upon him
and his companions and they fell to the earth. Paul
heard the voice of Christ. The Christ spoke to him
and told him what to do. He yielded himself to the
Lord and followed his instructions. He met the
Christ, recognized the Christ, believed the Christ,
accepted the Christ and was made into a new man
by the Christ.

2. SUCH HEAVENLY VISION SENDS THE SAVED

Paul was then informed by the messenger of the
Lord: "For thou shalt be his witness unto all men
of what thou hast seen and heard" (Acts 22:15).
Christ told Paul "I have appeared to thee for this
purpose, to make thee a minister and a witness both
of these things which thou hast seen and of those
things in the which I will appear unto thee." Paul
became the messenger of Christ to the Gentile world.
He was sent "To open their eyes, and to turn them

[75]

from darkness to light, and from the power of Satan
unto God, that they may receive forgiveness of
sins" (Acts 26:18). The saved Paul was sent by the
Saviour to witness for him.

3. SUCH HEAVENLY VISION SUSTAINS IN SERVICE

As Paul witnessed for Christ wherever he went,
he was sustained constantly by the vision of Christ
which he had on the way to Damascus. This experience encouraged, enriched, and ennobled his life
in every moment. He was sustained constantly in
all service of teaching, preaching, writing, organizing, and suffering by the presence of the Christ by
his side.

4. SUCH HEAVENLY VISION SEEKS SATISFACTION

When Paul met the Saviour three consuming
anxieties were born within his heart. His first desire was that he might know Christ perfectly. The
second was that he might become like him. The
third was that he might make him known to other
men. This heavenly vision ever led Paul forward
to the day when he could say, "For I am now ready
to be offered, and the time of my departure is at
hand" (2 Tim. 4:6).

As the heavenly vision saved and sent and sustained the great apostle, may it also come into the
lives of millions of others and do as much for each
one of them.

A PRAYER FOR GUIDANCE IN LIFE'S WAY

Make thy way straight before my face. Psalm 5:8.

In verse seven of this fifth Psalm is recorded two promises of the psalmist: one, that he would enter the house of the Lord; and two, that he would worship in faith toward his holy Temple. In verse eight there are two prayers: one, he prays the Lord to lead him in righteousness because of his enemies; and two, he prays the Lord to guide him in the right way. We call attention to this last prayer. It is a prayer for guidance along the way of life.

1. IT MUST BE A PREPARED WAY

"Make." The way would lead through trouble. It would be difficult unless some preparation was made. The Lord would make the way. He could make a way of deliverance from enemies, of overcoming difficulties, of enduring hardships, of escaping pitfalls, and of progress in the march onward. When the way is prepared by the Lord it is well done and right. It will be possible to travel the way prepared by the Lord.

2. IT MUST BE THE LORD'S WAY

"Thy way." As the weary traveler goes on with faith in God, he should be able to say, "This is the Lord's way and I will go on in it." It may be a way of sorrow but if it is of the Lord it will enrich the life. It may be a struggle to go on, but even this will give strength by the help of the Lord. Hardships, difficulties, temptations, and trials borne for the Lord and for his sake will refine and enrich character. Be sure it is the Lord's way and then be willing to walk in it faithfully.

3. IT MUST BE A STRAIGHT WAY

"Straight." This would not necessarily mean that the way would be as a straight line, with all crooks and curves taken out. It would mean that the way would be true to a correct course and that God's person would keep this ideal before him at all times. It would mean that the way of life would always conform to justice and rectitude and uprightness. The straight way must be properly ordered and correctly arranged. It is the way of righteousness. It is straight to God and his glory. Walk ye in it.

4. IT MUST BE A SERENE WAY

"Before my face." The Lord would make the way of life before us so clear and bright that there would be no mistake in it. The clear, steady light of the Lord would shine on the way to make it certain for his believer so he could say, "It is of the Lord and I must walk in it, come what may."

The Lord will abundantly bless the life that will follow faithfully in his way. Know the way of the Lord. Seek his will and follow his guidance and holy heights will be attained.

PRAYER THAT AVAILS

*The effectual fervent prayer of a righteous man
availeth much.* James 5:16.

In prayer there is power, for true prayer must be
unto the God of all power. This text is a positive
statement about prayer. It calls attention to the
man of prayer, the manner of prayer, and the result
of prayer.

1. THE MAN OF PRAYER MUST BE RIGHTEOUS

"A righteous man." The person who prays effectively must be righteous. To be righteous is to be
found in the right. The righteous person is right
with God, and he will be found in the right with all
men—in the home, church, community, nation, and
nations. He will be right in his thoughts, desires,
purposes, character, and conduct. A righteous man
will have no reason to be ashamed or embarrassed
in any company anywhere. He will have a hearty
welcome at the throne of grace. Live the righteous
life and win the right to enter the presence of the
Father on wings of prayer.

2. THE MANNER OF PRAYER MUST BE FERVENT

' "The effectual fervent prayer." The manner of
prayer must be earnest. It will be fervent suppli-
cation. The fervent prayer will be serious, sincere,
and submissive. It must be persistent, personal,
and powerful. It must be faithful and forceful.
Such prayer will be guided by the Holy Spirit and
offered in the name of Christ. It will be for the

[79]

glory of God and the good of men. Such eager and earnest prayer will reach the Father and bring down his power and connect it with the problems of men. "Lord, teach us to pray."

3. The Result of Prayer Will Be Pleasing

"Availeth much." The Lord God will hear the fervent prayer of a righteous man and answer it. Such prayer will avail and achieve. It will work and win. It will bring power and pleasure. It will accomplish for God and man. It will set the heart of man attune with the music of heaven. It will enrich and ennoble life. It will cause the blessings of God to flow abundantly into the life of men. The results of fervent prayer are too many to enumerate. They are more than can be counted. Yet the Heavenly Father invites us to come boldly to his throne of grace for his abundant blessings. What love! What joy! What power!

Be the righteous man. Pray the fervent prayer. See the power of God. Experience the glory of heaven. Use the power of prayer.

PRAYER WITH POWER

Prayer was made earnestly of the church unto God for him. Acts 12:5 (ASV).

This text is a good example of the prayer life of the Christians and church members of early days, and the result of the prayer. It is a good example for Christians of today to follow. Note the following things about this text:

1. THIS PRAYER WAS PROPER

"Prayer was made." It is always right for Christians to pray. They should pray at all times about all things and in all places. It was natural on this occasion for these Christians to pray. Prayer should be the desire of all Christians. It is right to pray in hours of success as well as in times of trouble and failure.

2. THIS PRAYER WAS TO THE RIGHT SOURCE

"Unto God." To whom can we go? These Christians prayed unto God in an hour of trouble. The Lord waits to hear his people pray. He is the God of grace and power. He has all power and will use it for his people. There is no other person to whom prayer can be made. All other sources of prayer avail nothing. Pray unto God. "Our Father, who art in heaven."

3. THIS PRAYER WAS BY THE RIGHT PEOPLE

"Of the church." The people who prayed on this occasion were Christians. They knew the Lord.

They believed in his power. They were members of the church. On other occasions they had gone to the mercy seat and were not turned away. Their hope was in God and they reached his power through prayer. This world is in need of Christians now who can go to the throne of grace and bring down the power of God and connect it with the problems of men.

4. This Prayer Was in the Right Spirit

"Earnestly." These church members prayed earnestly. They prayed without ceasing. They were sincere. Their prayer was eager and anxious. They agonized before the Lord. The Holy Spirit prompted the people with the right desire and purpose. The Lord will not turn such hearts away without granting the right answer. Pray earnestly, anxiously, and continuously.

5. This Prayer Was for the Right Person

"For him." Peter was in prison. He had been placed there for preaching Christ. He was bound to two soldiers. He was in trouble, thinking death might be his lot as it had come to James. Only the Lord could help. The Christians prayed unto God for Peter. It is right to pray for people who are in trouble. These Christians prayed unto God definitely for the deliverance of Peter from prison and the hands of Herod, and the Lord heard and answered and delivered him. "The effectual fervent prayer of a righteous man availeth much" (James 5:16).

6. This Prayer Was Rewarded with the Right Answer

The Lord sent his angel of mercy to the prison

and he found Peter sleeping between two soldiers.
The angel aroused Peter, loosed him, assisted him in
dressing, and led him out of prison and the hands
of Herod and to the house of prayer. The Lord answers prayer. He hears his people as they pray.

Learn the secret of prayer that has power with
God and engage in it earnestly and continuously for
his glory and his people.

PRAYING PETER OUT OF PRISON

Peter therefore was kept in prison: but prayer was made without ceasing of the church unto God for him. Acts 12:5.

We see in this chapter how Peter was placed in prison and how the members of the church prayed him out of prison. Note the reasons, the record, and the result of prayer.

1. THE REASON FOR PRAYER IS STATED

At this time King Herod stretched forth his hand to persecute certain members of the church. It is time for people to pray when rulers in high places begin to persecute Christians and the church. Many such rulers persecute Christianity by cruel neglect.

James the brother of John and a leader in the cause of Christ and the church was slain with the sword. He was not the last to die for the sake of Christ. Woe is upon people who deal thus with the Lord's people.

Peter, a leader of Christians, was placed in prison no doubt with the full intention of taking his life eventually. The Lord can intervene and upset the plans of wicked people when his followers rightly approach him.

2. THE RECORD OF PRAYER IS MADE

When Peter was placed in prison the members of the church at Jerusalem became alarmed and greatly concerned and set themselves to pray "for him." The prayers of the people were definite and most

[84]

earnest for Peter's release. Effectual praying must be definite. They prayed for Peter by name.

The praying was continuous. "Prayer was made without ceasing." Day and night, and day after day and night after night, the people prayed in the home of Mary, a devout member of the church whose home was ever open for the Lord's people to do the Lord's work.

The praying was "unto God." That is the right and only source. Who else can hear and answer prayer? The Lord is always willing and ready and anxious to hear the earnest prayers of his people. He will speak to those who will take time to listen.

3. THE RESULT OF PRAYER IS RECORDED

Three direct results of prayer are stated here. The Lord sent an angel to effect every detail in the release of Peter from prison, where he was guarded by many soldiers, and to guide him to the house of prayer and to restore him to the people and the service of the Lord. The Lord will hear and answer prayer. There is power in prayer.

The person who would punish the people of the Lord and persecute the church came to a most horrible end. The angel of the Lord smote Herod "and he was eaten of worms and gave up the ghost" (Acts 12:23). It is a fearful thing for any person to oppose God and his cause. Ruin is the only end for such people.

The cause of the Lord was promoted. "The word of God grew and multiplied" (Acts 12:24). The power of God as a result of the prayers of his people can defeat all plans of enemies and cause his Word to prosper.

The world is in grave need now of praying men who can reach up and take hold of the power of God and bring it down and connect it with the problems of men. Let us pray. Pray unto God without ceasing and see his glorious works among men.

THE PREACHER'S PLIGHT

Then Peter said, Silver and gold have I none; but such as I have give I thee. Acts 3:6.

This is a wonderful story in the third chapter of Acts. In modern language, Peter as the preacher was "on the spot" as he healed the lame man, spoke to the people, and faced the court. See what he said and did in such condition.

1. THE PREACHER EXPRESSED POVERTY

"Silver and gold have I none." Peter had long since turned his back on material wealth and given himself to things eternal. He no longer had a desire to make money. He was not encumbered with worldly wealth. He had a more glorious goal, and was giving himself to a more worthy work. The preacher was poor in things of the earth. Silver and gold were only minor things as compared with what he had found. Blessed is the man who can rise above the things of the earth.

2. THE PREACHER EXPERIENCED POSSESSIONS

"But such as I have." This preacher had something far better than silver and gold. He had eternal life in Christ. He had the love of God in his heart. He had Christ in his soul. He had the passion of the Lord in his life. He had an earnest desire to help the lame man. He had the spirit of God dominating his life. He had the best gift. He had the most worthy wealth. He had Christ and God and the Holy Spirit. He had eternal riches. His possessions were really all that a true heart could ask or desire for this life and the life to come. He was immensely wealthy with riches from heaven. How great his riches! How happy his life! How powerful his word!

3. THE PREACHER EXERCISED POWER

"Give I thee. In the name of Jesus Christ of Nazareth rise up and walk." This preacher had power. He had the power of God at his command. He was able to use the power of God in Christ to give strength to the man who had been lame for forty years. What power! It was the power of the God of the universe. It was power to give physical strength. It was power to change the body, the heart, and the life. Blessed is the man who has the power of God and uses it for the glory of God and the good of mankind.

4. THE PREACHER EXPLAINED PROPHECY

When the man who had been lame was healed and went "into the temple walking, and leaping, and praising God . . . and . . . held Peter and John, all the people ran together unto them in the porch that is called Solomon's, greatly wondering." When Peter saw this he realized it was a good time to explain the gospel of Christ to the people. He effectively pointed out that before their eyes had been fulfilled "those things, which God before had shewed by the mouth of all his prophets, that Christ should suffer" (Acts 3:18). He then called on the people to repent of their sin and believe in Christ, showing them that "all the prophets from Samuel and those that follow after, as many as have spoken, have likewise foretold of these days" (Acts 3:24). The preacher was mighty in his proclamation of the gospel.

May the Lord give the world more preachers who possess the riches of heaven and use the power of God for the proclamation of the gospel for the lift of humanity.

THE LORD'S PRECIOUS PROMISES

I am with thee, and will keep thee in all the places whither thou goest.   Genesis 28:15.

In his dream, Jacob saw a ladder reaching from earth to heaven. He heard the Lord speak the words of this text to him from the top of the ladder. This is a precious promise. It is precious in its origin because it comes from God. It is precious in its objective because of what it would mean to Jacob and to all people who will hear it. We note the following phases of the promise.

1. The Lord Has Promised His Presence

"I am with thee." The Lord promised Jacob that he would be with him in every act, in every movement, and in every step of the way before him. Jacob was well supported when he had the presence of the Lord along with him. The Lord says to his own, "I am with thee." He will go before his own. He will be behind his own. He will stand by his own. It is wonderful to have the consciousness of his presence. He will be true to every promise he has made to his servants. The Lord is with us. We can trust him. We can depend upon his promises. We can stand on the promises of God. He will keep his promises to us.

2. The Lord Has Promised His Power

"And will keep thee." The power of the Lord will save from sin, direct from every danger, protect in every peril, guide to his glory, seek for success, and lead to the top of the ladder in every attainment for his cause. His power is with us. He promises all the power that we will need to accomplish his purposes in life. His gracious power is sufficient to meet every demand and to satisfy every need that we will have on every occasion as we seek to serve in his kingdom. Depend on the power of the Lord.

3. THE LORD HAS PROMISED HIS PROTECTION

"In all the places whither thou goest." The Lord had a plan for the life of Jacob. He promised to lead Jacob in the way of right and righteousness. His hand guided Jacob every step of the way. His presence and power assured him of every need. The Lord has a plan for every life. He desires to work out this plan in every life as he worked it out in the life of Jacob. He will do even more for the life in this day than he did for Jacob, because his revelation to man is full now, and his grace is abundant and sufficient through Christ and the Holy Spirit.

Walking in the presence of the Lord, using the power of the Lord, trusting him for his protection and providential care, and being assured that he will work out his plan in our life, we can well afford to trust the Lord and depend on every promise he has made.

REPENTANCE

Except ye repent, ye shall all likewise perish.
Luke 13:3.

Earnest, definite, scriptural messages on this subject are needed now possibly more than on any other subject.

The Bible has much to say about repentance. The first text of John the Baptist was "Repent ye: for the kingdom of heaven is at hand" (Matt. 3:2). Jesus put it stronger, "Except ye repent, ye shall all likewise perish." Peter preached repentance on the day of Pentecost. Paul preached to Jews and Greeks "repentance toward God, and faith toward our Lord Jesus Christ" (Acts 20:21).

Preachers of other days delivered burning messages on this subject. Whitfield thundered out the necessity for repentance. The power of Wesley's message was repentance. The thrill of Moody's story was repentance and this is the message that made Edwards great in our land. Preachers now should tell men that they have sinned against God and call them to repentance.

What is repentance? A brief answer is "Repentance is being so conscious of sin and so sorry for sin that the guilty will by the help of God turn away from sin to Christ by faith." This definition suggests three essential steps in repentance.

1. IT IS CONSCIOUSNESS OF SIN

No one will repent of sin until he is painfully conscious of sin. Sin makes a mighty attack on all men and they yield and it leaves its mark. Sin has left its mark on every home and in every nation that has been established. Sin takes the child from mother's arms and drops it down to ruin and breaks her heart. Sin is against man and against God and demands repentance and atonement. God is pure and holy and has a holy and pure standard for the people of the earth. To fall beneath this standard is to sin against God.

2. IT IS SORROW FOR SIN

Before the guilty will repent of sin there must be sorrow for sin against God. This must be godly sorrow. It is more than the sorrow that comes when man or the law knows the sin. It must be deep and pungent and painful remorse of soul that one has sinned against the pure, just, and holy heart of a loving God. There must be a broken and contrite heart before there is any genuine repentance. It must be a sorrow that will bite. This kind of sorrow will cause distress of soul. It is like a gnawing pain. It is agony of soul caused by a sense of guilt. Such sorrow will lead a soul to true repentance.

3. IT IS TURNING FROM SIN

When the soul is painfully conscious of sin and truly sorry for sin, it is then ready to turn from sin. It will realize it must turn or burn, repent or perish. God will have only a quitting repentance. That means that if a man is a profane swearer and repents, he gives up profanity forever. If a man is a drunkard and repents, he will drink no more. If a person is immoral and repents, he gives up immorality for all time. Repentance is not only a heart broken because of sin, but a life broken from sin. Repentance is declaring unending warfare on sin. It is the act of the prodigal when he said, "I will arise and go to my father," and he went and made all things right.

The soul turns from sin by repentance and to Christ by faith. Without faith there can be no possession of real spiritual life. Faith is essential to true repentance. This Paul emphasized when he said, "Repentance toward God and faith toward our Lord Jesus Christ." The soul must lay hold on the promises of God and believe and accept Jesus Christ, the Saviour from sin. "He that believeth on the Son hath everlasting life" (John 3:36). "Believe on the Lord Jesus Christ, and thou shalt be saved" (Acts 16:31).

With consciousness of sin and sorrow for sin, turn from sin to God and walk in holy fellowship with him. Preach it powerfully. Preach it until it is practiced.

THE REQUIREMENTS OF THE LORD

What doth the Lord thy God require of thee, but to fear the Lord thy God, to walk in all his ways, and to love him, and to serve the Lord thy God . . ., to keep the commandments of the Lord . . .? Deuteronomy 10:12-13.

The words of this text were spoken to the children of Israel by Moses, but all through the Bible we see that they are the words of the Lord and that he requires these things of his people in all ages. See what the Lord requires of his own.

1. THE LORD REQUIRES FAITH. "TO FEAR THE LORD THY GOD."

The word "fear" in this text, as in other similar uses in the Old Testament, means faith or trust. The Lord is eager that his people shall believe in him, have faith in him, and trust him. His people must believe in the eternal purpose of God, have faith in the plan of God, and trust the providential acts of God. God requires faith. Have faith in God.

2. THE LORD REQUIRES LOYALTY. "TO WALK IN ALL HIS WAYS."

The Lord reserves the right to lead his people. He may lead where the way is dark and rough, or where there is no water or food, or where fierce enemies may attack, but if the Lord leads every necessity will be abundantly provided. The Lord's people must walk in the way of justice, righteousness, holiness, benevolence, and mercy. They must walk not only in his way but in all his ways. In his ways and with his leadership all may be happy and prosperous.

3. THE LORD REQUIRES LOVE. "AND TO LOVE HIM."

The Lord requires that his people love him supremely. They are to love the Lord with all their heart, with all their soul, with all their mind, and with all their strength. Some people love pleasure, wealth, life, relatives, and other things more than they love the Lord. The servant of the Lord must love the Lord more than all else. When love for the Lord is supreme, love for the Bible, the kingdom, the church, and worship and fellowship divine will naturally follow. God requires love. Love him supremely.

4. THE LORD REQUIRES SERVICE. "AND TO SERVE THE LORD THY GOD."

When people have faith in God and walk in his ways, and love him supremely, they will desire to serve him to the very best of their ability and knowledge. The wicked world sorely needs the service of the Lord's people in this hour. The hungry are to be fed, the thirsty must have water, the sorrowing should be comforted, the stranger needs to be entertained, the sick needs a helping hand, the prisoner needs encouragement, the sinner must be saved, the wayward must be brought back to the Lord. The field is ripe unto harvest. The reapers are few. The Lord needs the fruitful service of his people.

5. THE LORD REQUIRES OBEDIENCE. "TO KEEP THE COMMANDMENTS OF THE LORD."

This reference probably applies to the Ten Commandments but as revelation came to its fulness other commandments were given to Christians. The Lord requires obedience. His people must obey his will, and do his work in his way. His people are to love him supremely, and to love their neighbors as themselves, and to proclaim the gospel to all people of all nations. Obey the commands of the Lord.

Come to know the requirements of the Lord and seek to live the fulness of the expectation of the Lord God at all times.

RECEIVING SALVATION

A certain ruler came to Jesus and said, "Good Master, what shall I do to inherit eternal life?" (Luke 18:18). The people on the day of Pentecost asked. "What shall we do?" (Acts 2:37). The jailer in Philippi on being aroused from sleep asked Paul and Silas, "Sirs, what must I do to be saved?" (Acts 16:30).

The Bible answers to these questions show that no individual can do anything to merit or deserve eternal life. It is revealed, however, that individuals can do certain things to receive eternal life. We call attention to these things:

1. THE SOUL CAN LOOK UNTO THE LORD

"Look unto me, and be ye saved, all the ends of the earth: for I am God, and there is none else (Isa. 45:22). As Israel was called upon to look unto the Lord for salvation, so now are all people of all the nations. Souls can look to the Lord for eternal life.

2. THE SOUL CAN SEEK THE LORD

"Seek ye the Lord while he may be found, call ye upon him while he is near" (Isa. 55:6). The Lord is near every soul for every person lives and moves and has his being in him. The soul that desires eternal life has only to seek the Lord and he will be found ready to give life.

3. THE SOUL CAN BELIEVE ON THE LORD

"Believe on the Lord Jesus Christ, and thou shalt be saved, and thy house" (Acts 16:31). The reply to the seeker is to believe on the Lord Jesus Christ. The soul must believe that the Lord is and that he has power to save and is willing to save and will save. The soul can believe on the Lord.

4. THE SOUL CAN CALL UPON THE LORD

"For whosoever shall call upon the name of the Lord shall be saved" (Rom. 10:13). Those who believe on the Lord can call upon him; in fact there is no one else to whom a lost person can go.

5. THE SOUL CAN REPENT OF SIN

"Except ye repent, ye shall all likewise perish" (Luke 13:5). These are the words of Jesus. Paul used the same thought when he said to the Jews and Greeks, "Repentance toward God" (Acts 20:21). It is repentance or ruin; it is turn or burn. Repentance is essential. The soul that is conscious of sin and has a godly sorrow for sin will turn away from sin. This is true repentance.

6. THE SOUL CAN RECEIVE THE LORD

"But as many as received him, to them gave he power to become the sons of God, even to them that believe on his name" (John 1:12). This is the test. When the soul looks to him and seeks him, believing in his ability and calls upon him as it turns away from sin, it can receive eternal life by giving Christ welcome.

7. THE SOUL CAN CONFESS THE LORD

"But whosoever shall deny me before men, him will I also deny before my Father which is in heaven" (Matt. 10:33). When a soul has received the Lord it will be happy to confess his name before men.

8. THE SOUL CAN OBEY THE LORD

"If ye love me, keep my commandments" (John 14:15). When the soul receives the Lord and eternal life which he gives, it will be a joy to keep his commandments and to do his service.

Look unto the Lord seeking eternal life which he offers. By faith call upon him and receive this life as you turn away from sin by repentance, and then obey the Lord in his service.

SEEKING THE LORD

Seek ye the Lord while he may be found, call ye upon him while he is near. Isaiah 55:6.

This text is a call to all men to seek and find and believe and embrace the Lord God of heaven and earth. Possibly there is no more timely text for this world in this day than this one. Let us note:

1. THE LORD IS NEAR

"While he is near." The Lord God is everywhere. We cannot go from his spirit nor flee from his presence. He is in the heavens and in the earth, on the sea and the land, in the light and the darkness. The psalmist could not find a place to hide from God (Psalm 139:7-12). No one can hide from him. He is very near every soul, as near as the air or light or darkness. He gives life, for we live and move and have our being in him. Recognize the Lord for he is near. Invite him into your life.

2. THE LORD MAY BE FOUND

"While he may be found." One of the greatest blessings of life is that the Lord may be found by the seeking heart. He is at the side of every lonely soul, waiting to be recognized and invited into the heart. By faith the soul can see him, hear him, love him, and live for him. When he is invited to come into the heart he will enter with life and love and light. He will give grace and goodness, meekness and mercy, joy and justice, holiness and happiness, peace and perfection. Let him into your life while he may be found.

3. THE LORD MUST BE SOUGHT

"Seek ye the Lord." The God of this universe has sought men through the ages. He has revealed himself to men as they were able and willing to comprehend. He is eager to give to everyone the blessings of life abundantly. Yet the Lord awaits men to recognize their need for him and to seek his blessings. Over and over again and again in the Bible men are admonished to seek the Lord. He will quickly hear the call of men and respond to their seeking. Men should seek the Lord. "Seek and ye shall find."

It is a joy to know that the Lord can be found if only we will seek him for he is so very near each soul and is eager to enter and to bless.

SOME EFFECTS OF SIN

*God hath said, Ye shall not eat of it, neither shall
ye touch it lest ye die.* Genesis 3:3.

This story of the sin of man as recorded in Genesis 3:1-24 is the beginning of the dark history and horrible record of sin in the world. What sin did to man in those days it has been doing through the years. Note the following:

1. SIN MADE MAN AFRAID OF GOD

When Adam and Eve had disobeyed the command of the Lord they sought to hide themselves from God. Sin made them afraid of God, and man has been afraid of God from that day until this. Sinful people are often afraid even of the servants of God.

2. SIN KEEPS PEOPLE FROM THE PLACE OF WORSHIP

It was the habit of Adam and Eve to meet the Lord in the garden and to worship him there. The record states that the Lord God came to the garden in the cool of the day, and Adam and Eve, his wife, hid themselves from the presence of the Lord. Sinful people seek to hide themselves from his presence.

3. SIN BREAKS FELLOWSHIP BETWEEN MAN AND GOD

It was the custom of Adam and Eve to have fellowship with the Lord in the garden constantly. When sin came into their lives and they had disobeyed the Lord this fellowship was broken. And

when the Lord came to the garden again he called
unto Adam and Eve, saying, "Where art thou?"
Sin also breaks the fellowship between man and man
in every relationship of life.

4. SIN SHUTS MAN OUT OF THE HIGHEST GOOD IN LIFE

When sin came into the life of Adam and Eve they
were cast out of Eden—a place of joy and happiness.
Swords were placed at the entrance of Eden to pre-
vent their return to this happy place. Sin always
separates man from that which is high and holy in
life.

5. SIN MUST BE PUNISHED

Sin called down a curse on all connected with this
disobedience of the Lord. Eternal curse was pro-
nounced upon the serpent, the woman, and Adam as
punishment for the sin committed. There is a way
out of sin. It is by grace through faith in Christ.

A SINFUL MAN AND THE SEEKING SAVIOUR

For the Son of man is come to seek and to save that which was lost. Luke 19:10.

The first ten verses of this chapter of Luke give a remarkable account of Jesus dealing with a sinful man. The event illustrates the fact stated in the text, that Jesus Christ is the Saviour seeking for, and saving, lost men. Note three things in the passage.

1. THE NATURE OF THE MAN IS GIVEN

Among the things mentioned about Zaccheus, we name these four:

(1) He was a publican. In fact he was chief among the publicans. He gathered from the people the taxes for the Roman Government. He was therefore despised by the people. This was a serious barrier for him.

(2) He was rich. He had secured his wealth by taking it from the people by false accusation. He collected more than was required for taxes and kept it for himself. He was rich only in material things.

(3) He was small. He was little of stature. This was a disadvantage to him in seeing Jesus for he could not see over the crowds of people about him. A great soul may reside in a small body.

(4) He was a sinner. He was a sinner in the sight of God. This was his record in the community. The people knew his sin and accused him publicly. He realized his sinful condition and later did

[105]

something about it.　There is always hope for a sinner who will seek Jesus.

2. THE MOVEMENTS OF THE MAN ARE MENTIONED

Four things are said clearly here about the activities of this lost man.

(1) He had a desire to see Jesus.　This desire might have been aroused by curiosity, but his actions show that the desire was deep and must have been to find one who could save him from his sin.　Sinners will never be saved until they have a sincere desire to be saved.

(2) He made an effort to see Jesus.　He ran before the crowds out on the road leading out to Jerusalem and climbed up into a sycamore tree to see Jesus as he approached.　The sinner who seeks Jesus will be sure to find him, for he is also seeking the lost.

(3) He received Jesus joyfully.　When Jesus stood under the tree and called him by name, he made haste and came down and received him with great joy.　Happy is the soul that responds to the loving invitation of the Lord.

(4) He confessed his sin to Jesus.　He had not been with the Saviour very long before he began to tell Jesus of his sin and how he was willing to give it up and to make right all of the wrongs of the past. This is the best evidence of turning from sin to Christ.

3. THE RESPONSE OF JESUS IS RECORDED

The attitude of Jesus toward Zaccheus is his attitude toward all sinners everywhere.

(1) Jesus knew the man.　As he stood under the tree and looked up to the man, he called him by

name. He not only knew his name but he knew his character. He has all knowledge. He knows the heart of every man.

(2) Jesus honored the man. He went home with this man, even though the people knew him to be a sinner. He was honored above all other men in the crowd. It is the glory of the Christ that he came to seek and to save sinners.

(3) Jesus listened to the man. When they were in the home, Jesus did not do much of the talking, for soon Zaccheus was telling him all about all of his sin and how he wanted to get rid of it and to make all things right with all people. Tell it to Jesus.

(4) Jesus saved the man. After the man had confessed his sin, Jesus said unto him: "This day is salvation come to this house." Jesus said it and I believe it. The Saviour saves sinful men who repent and accept.

All sinful men everywhere will be able to find salvation in the seeking Saviour. Seek him. Believe him. Accept him. Rejoice in him.

THE SHEPHERDS AND THE LORD'S MESSAGE

Make a study of the passage of Scripture from the eighth to the twentieth verses of the second chapter of Luke and find there the many things about the shepherds and the Lord's message. It will be found that the shepherds heard, believed, verified, appropriated, and proclaimed the Lord's message.

1. THE SHEPHERDS HEARD THE LORD'S MESSAGE

"And there were in the same country shepherds abiding in the field, keeping watch over their flock by night" (v. 8). To deliver a message to men; he delivered it to lowly shepherds rather than to the king in the palace. These men were busy in the line of duty, "keeping watch over their flock by night." This same action of the Lord in calling busy men is seen when he spoke to Moses keeping the flock of Jethro (Ex. 3:2); Saul looking for his father's animals (1 Sam. 9:1-11); Isaiah worshiping in the Temple (Isa. 6:1-8); David as he cared for the flock in the field (1 Sam. 16:11-13); Simon and Andrew as they were casting their nets (Mark 1:16); James and John as they were mending their nets (Mark 1:19). This seems to sanction the idea that busy people are more likely to do things when called upon.

2. THE SHEPHERDS BELIEVED THE LORD'S MESSAGE

"Let us now go even unto Bethlehem, and see this thing which is come to pass, which the Lord hath made known unto us" (v. 15). When the shepherds heard the voice of the angel, they believed the message which he delivered. They believed that the event of which he spoke had occurred and they accepted the message of the angel as to the place of its occurrence and as to the Person who was born. They believed the message which was delivered by the angel. Blessed are those who believe the Lord's message.

3. THE SHEPHERDS VERIFIED THE LORD'S MESSAGE

"And they came with haste, and found Mary, and Joseph, and the babe lying in a manger" (v. 16). It is intimated elsewhere that these men sought to find the record in prophecy as to where the Christ child would be born and having verified it they went to Bethlehem. In this city of David they actually found the mother, and Joseph, and the Babe even as the angel had told them. As the star led them and the glory of the Lord shone round about the shepherds, the sight of the Babe must have been more glorious than they had anticipated. Christianity has always invited thorough investigation in the words "Come and see."

4. THE SHEPHERDS APPROPRIATED THE LORD'S MESSAGE

"The shepherds returned, glorifying and praising God for all the things that they had heard and seen" (v. 20). When the shepherds had heard the message and accepted it and verified it, they appropriated it into their own lives. Immediately there was great joy and they began to glorify and praise the Lord for revealing his message unto them and leading them to actually see the young child. The joy of Christianity is one of its greatest characteristics, as is always seen when a person finds Christ, accepts him, and seeks to live his life over.

5. THE SHEPHERDS PROCLAIMED THE LORD'S MESSAGE

"They made known abroad the saying which was told them" (v. 17). The shepherds not only heard the message and believed it and appropriated it into their own lives, but they did the thing which Christianity expects of a believer. They proclaimed the message to other people. In fancy we can see these men stopping with every person on the way and at the wayside inn and other places to gather the people together and tell them of the wonderful event which had occurred, and of the things which they had actually seen and heard. We can imagine them back in their own homes gathering the family together to relate the message of the Christ child. So it is when people find the Christ, they joyfully seek to make him known to others.

The world's great Christmas message is that of the Christ. The greatest blessing to the heart is to hear, believe, verify, appropriate, and proclaim the message of the Christ.

A GOOD SOLDIER OF JESUS CHRIST

Thou therefore endure hardness, as a good soldier of Jesus Christ. 2 Timothy 2:3.

The life of the soldier was familiar to Timothy to whom Paul wrote this epistle. Paul therefore used the soldier's life as a parallel to the Christian life. The life of the soldier is familiar to our people in this day. It is a good time to think about a good soldier of Jesus Christ. We note a few of the requirements.

1. A Good Soldier Must Be a Citizen of the Kingdom

A person enters the kingdom of God only by the spiritual birth which comes by grace through faith in Christ. When one is thus a citizen of the kingdom, he becomes a child of God and a subject of the Ruler of the spiritual kingdom. He should seek to learn the principles of the kingdom and to be true and loyal to these under all circumstances. Believers compose the army of the Lord and Christ is the head of this army.

2. A Good Soldier Must Be a Volunteer

Citizens of the kingdom of God can easily see the great need for service. The doors of opportunity are opened wide. The Master calls for ready and willing hearts to serve in every place of need. Blessed is the person who sees the place of service and hears the call of Christ, and gladly offers himself, voluntarily, to do all he can for defending or advancing the kingdom of God. When Christ calls, his followers should be ready to say, "Here am I, send me."

3. A GOOD SOLDIER MUST BE CLASSIFIED

Many places are to be filled in the service of the Lord. Christ needs willing workers to preach, teach, visit, read, sing, pray, comfort, encourage, strengthen, build, guide, and many other types of service. Every soldier of Jesus Christ is given some special inclination and ability and can serve best in the particular place for which he is fitted by native ability and acquired skill. The Lord will lead each anxious and prayerful heart to the right type of service and place for service. Good soldiers of Christ will find their place for best service.

4. A GOOD SOLDIER MUST BE TRAINED FOR SERVICE

Training for service is essential. In war, men are highly trained to kill and to destroy. To care for the physical body, we seek the best trained surgeons, doctors, dentists, and nurses. Those who are to teach are required to take years of training. Surely those who are to deal with the soul, which is eternal, must have the best preparation. Good soldiers of Christ Jesus will do all in their power to become well trained for their high and holy task. It is necessary to be trained. It is possible for everyone to be trained for his specific task. Take time and put forth every effort to this end. Be a trained soldier of Christ.

5. A Good Soldier Must Be Obedient to Christ

Those who love Christ and his kingdom supremely will find it easy to be obedient to Christ. It is possible for the good soldier to know the will of Christ. When one knows his will, it will be a joy to do it. He commands his disciples to wait in prayer for the power and then to go and make disciples of all people of all nations of all the world. When disciples are made, they are to be taught to observe all things which were taught by the Christ. No one who loves the Lord can be happy in anything less than full obedience. Disciples of Christ must be true to the commands of Christ.

6. A Good Soldier Must Be Faithful to Duty

Faithfulness is required of a good soldier. This must be in the daily task. He will have no time to become entangled with the affairs of the world. He will often find hardships in the way. A good soldier will be faithful even if he loses his life in the act, but even in this the good soldier will receive the crown of life.

Be a good soldier of Jesus Christ. Find your work. Prepare yourself for it. Obey the Lord. Be faithful even unto death. Christ will reward the good soldier.

EVIDENCE OF SONSHIP

*As many as are led by the Spirit of God, these
are the sons of God.* Romans 8:14.

In this great text the relationship between the individual heart and the Spirit of God is clearly indi-
cated. Let us find at least three words of instruc-
tion from the sentiment and teaching found in the
text.

1. SONS MAY FIND THE PURPOSE OF THE SPIRIT

The New Testament clearly teaches that the Holy
Spirit is the agent of the new birth: "That which is
born of the Spirit is spirit." The purpose of the
Holy Spirit is also to convict the world of sin, and
of righteousness, and of judgment, to reveal eternal
truth, to testify of Christ, to comfort the sorrowing,
and to help the needy. The purpose of the Holy
Spirit of God is to seek to carry out the will of God
on earth in the hearts of men. Surely every soul
should desire to find the purpose and depend on the
power of the Holy Spirit.

2. SONS MAY FEEL THE POWER OF THE SPIRIT

"These are the sons of God." Children of God are
conscious of the presence of the Holy Spirit in cre-
ating a desire for eternal life and the power of the
Holy Spirit as the agent of the new birth, and the
work of the Holy Spirit in sustaining the spiritual
life. Only divine power, the power of God through
the work of the Holy Spirit, can so move on the
hearts of men. Also, it is by his power that we are

able to witness and serve effectively for the Lord. It is through his power that we can approach the throne of grace in an acceptable manner, for the Holy Spirit forms the right attitudes and desires in the human heart. Man needs to feel the power of the Holy Spirit in every move and movement for the Lord.

3. Sons May Follow the Presence of the Spirit

"As many as are led by the spirit." As we follow the leadership of the Spirit we show that we are the sons of God, and place ourselves where we may become effective in service for the Lord. As we follow the Spirit, we go in the right way, think the right thoughts, speak the right words, do the right things, walk the upward way, and accomplish the will of the Heavenly Father.

May the sons of God find the purpose of the Holy Spirit, feel the power of his presence, and follow his leading so that we may know and do the will of God on earth.

THINGS A WEAK MAN COULD DO

*A certain man was there, which had an infirmity
thirty and eight years.* John 5:5.

The man mentioned in this text was one of a great
multitude of afflicted people gathered at the pool of
Bethesda in Jerusalem seeking to be healed. We note
several things about this weak man which are mentioned in the passage.

1. THE MAN CONFESSED HIS WEAKNESS

"Sir, I have no man . . . to put me into the pool"
(v. 7). The man realized his weakness. He had
possibly grown weaker and weaker as the years
passed. All men live and move and have their being
in the God of the universe. Apart from him they
can do nothing. No sinner will be saved until he
realizes that he cannot save himself. No Christian
will be powerful in the service of the Lord until he
realizes that his strength must come from God.
Churches will become powerful when they realize
their weakness away from the Lord and look to him
for strength.

2. THE WEAK MAN CONFERRED WITH JESUS

"Jesus saw him lie, and knew that he had been
now a long time in that case" (v. 6). Jesus is always near when there is sin, suffering, sickness, or
sorrow. The man had his chance to talk with Jesus
and to tell him about his weakness. Every wicked
wayward man will have an opportunity to talk with
the Lord. Every weak, infirm, unsteady, ineffective

Christian will have his chance to talk with Jesus and to receive his strength. Just a talk with Jesus and a response to his loving mercy will make all things right. "Wilt thou be made whole?" Then look to Jesus. "The man was made whole." Jesus will do the same for you.

3. THE WEAK MAN OBEYED JESUS

"Immediately the man was made whole, and took up his bed, and walked" (v. 9). When Jesus would help the man, he refused to talk about his affliction and trouble and weakness and commanded him, "Rise, take up thy bed, and walk." The man responded immediately and arose and walked away with his bed. He exercised faith and courage and obeyed the command even though he did not know the Speaker, who disappeared in the crowd. The weak and weary and discouraged soul needs to obey the voice of the Lord. The limping, crippled, crawling Christian needs to hear the voice of power and to respond to it.

4. THE WEAK MAN HONORED JESUS

"Afterward Jesus findeth him in the temple, and said unto him, Behold, thou art made whole" (v. 14). The man did not go away leaping and rejoicing to spend his life in worldly pleasure or to doing questionable things which he had not been able to do, but he went into the Temple. It is assumed that the man desired to express his gratitude to God for his health and strength being restored. The remark of Jesus "thou art made whole" would confirm this. Even a weak man can be thankful to God for blessings and express this gratitude to God.

The weak man who was willing to confess his weakness, confer with Jesus, and obey him became whole and strong in Christ. It is possible for all weak men to have this experience.

THINK ON THY WAY

I thought on my ways. Psalm 119:59.

This passage of Scripture shows the necessity of sincere thought on the ways of life. Thought is essential to right decisions and duties in life. The mind is given to man to use. Thinking must be clear and correct. Note the blessings of right thinking.

1. RIGHT THINKING WILL REVEAL DIRECTION

"I thought on my ways." The inference is that the soul was on the wrong way. It was going the downward direction. Though the way of sin looks inviting, it is filled with iniquity and trouble. "The way of transgressors is hard" (Prov. 13:15). "The Lord knoweth the way of the righteous: but the way of the ungodly shall perish" (Psalm 1:6). "The wicked shall be turned into hell" (Psalm 9:17). The way of the wicked leads to eternal ruin. It is time for the transgressor, the ungodly, and the wicked to stop and think on their ways. Serious thought will sober the sinful soul.

2. RIGHT THINKING WILL REACH DECISION

"I turned my feet unto thy testimonies." The soul on the downward way saw the ruin ahead and the fatal end and took a serious thought and turned about-face and accepted the way of the Lord and went in it. No soul can do this without the convicting power of the Holy Spirit. When a soul is convinced of the error of the way and the need of the

Saviour, it can turn from sin by repentance and to Christ by faith and walk in the way of the Lord. Sincere, prayerful thought, guided by the Holy Spirit will turn any sinful soul to the Saviour. This decision is for Christ and eternity with him.

3. RIGHT THINKING WILL REVEAL DUTY

"I made haste, and delayed not to keep thy commandments." Much time has been lost. Much talent has been wasted. Many dangers are pursuing Much work must be done. Time must be redeemed. The Lord calls to duty. Many tasks await for doing. Souls and lives are to be saved before it is too late. Lessons must be taught. Songs must be sung. Truth must be proclaimed. Visits must be made. There is no time for the Christian to waste.

Sincere thinking will reveal direction, reach decision, and reveal duty. Think rightly. Think now.

THE WAY JESUS DID IT

Give ye them to eat. Matthew 14:16; Mark 6:37; Luke 9:13; John 6:11.

This marvelous miracle of our Master must have a new meaning for many in this day of world need of the spiritual message. The miracle is unusual in that it is the only one which is recorded in each of the Four Gospels. Also it evidently made the most profound impression on the people. It shows us how Jesus went about his work. See in it the following lessons.

1. JESUS RECOGNIZED THE NEED

"This is a desert place." "They have nothing to eat." "The time is now past." All day the people had been out in the mountain with Jesus without food. They were now hungry and would soon be faint. The need of food for the body on that occasion was no greater than the need for spiritual food for the soul in all the world now. Jesus now recognizes this great need and would have his disciples see it and do something about it.

2. JESUS REALIZED THE TASK

"We have here but five loaves, and two fishes" (Matt. 14:17). "What are they among so many?" (John 6:9). In the multitude "were about five thousand men, besides women and children" (Matt. 14:21). To feed this many people with the luncheon of the lad was no small task. It could be done only by the power of the Lord. In this same Christ there is sufficient spiritual food now for all the people of all the nations of all the world. The task is to get the message to the people.

3. JESUS ORGANIZED THE PEOPLE

"He commanded the multitude to sit down on the grass" (Matt. 14:19). "And they sat down in ranks, by hundreds, and by fifties" (Mark 6:40). Jesus believed in organization. He knew that great tasks can be accomplished only in this way. Here is definite authority of our Lord for organizing churches and missions and then these into departments and classes and groups for supplying the need of all. If we shall supply the gospel to all people now we must organize for it.

4. JESUS USED WHAT HE HAD

"Took the five loaves, and the two fishes." This was all that could be found in the desert place. It was all that Jesus had to use. It was all he needed. He could use this lunch and in his hands it could become ample to feed the multitude. Jesus expects us to use what we have and all that we have to feed a hungry world. Our little in his hands can be sufficient. He will use our hands and hearts, our lives and love for victory.

5. JESUS PRAYED TO THE FATHER

"He looked up to heaven, and blessed" (Mark 6:41). Even Jesus could not undertake this task without the help of the Father. He went about his work in prayer and was always successful. Is there a better way for us to begin any task? Pray as a life begins, when a home is established, as churches are organized, as missionaries are sent out, and when any task is undertaken for the Lord. There is power in prayer.

6. JESUS HAD FAITH TO SUCCEED

"He himself knew what he would do" (John 6:6). As Jesus took the loaves and fishes, he knew that he could feed the multitude with them. He went about his task with faith. Our Lord would have us go about his work in faith. When we know a task is going to be accomplished, we can do it more heartily. To do anything heartily, we must believe in it. It takes faith to feed the spiritual food to a hungry world. By faith in the power of God and the greatness of the gospel of Christ and the help of the Holy Spirit, it can be done.

7. JESUS USED HIS DISCIPLES

"Gave the loaves to the disciples, and the disciples to the multitude." What a joy to be able to help Jesus in his work! Yes, the Lord desires to use all who love him and believe in him for the progress of his work. He revealed his message to Paul and made him an apostle to the Gentiles. So in this day he sends his messengers to the lost people of the earth. Live so Christ can use you. Let life be lifted by his love through you.

8. JESUS BELIEVED IN ECONOMY

"He said unto his disciples, Gather up the fragments that remain, that nothing be lost" (John 6: 12). Jesus would not waste even a crumb. He would use for the progress of his kingdom every moment of time, every ounce of strength, every bit of talent of all believers. Do not waste time or talent but use all for the Lord.

If we shall go about the work of our Lord as Jesus did we will see glorious success in his name.

"WHAT DOTH THE LORD REQUIRE?"

What doth the Lord require of thee, but to do justly, and to love mercy, and to walk humbly with thy God? Micah 6:8.

Some years ago a wayward son of a mother in our congregation was suddenly snatched into eternity in an automobile wreck. When the mother talked to me about the funeral service she requested me to use this text, intimating that repentance toward and faith in Jesus Christ are not essential to salvation. Micah in this text mentions God's requirements, but has nothing to say about God's gifts. In this day of full revelation of God through Christ, the requirements of this text can be met only through repentance toward God and faith in the Lord Jesus Christ. In this light we look at God's requirements.

Micah covers in this text in a condensed form substantially the same ground that Moses does in the Decalogue, only Moses began with the true foundation in a true relation to God, which is most important, and leads on to the true relation to man. Micah begins with the lesser, the purely human, and leads on to that which is the center and source of all.

1. THE LORD REQUIRES JUSTICE

"To do justly." God does require justice. Only a righteous person can do the right in every relationship in life. True righteousness comes to man from God through Christ. Righteousness is an element of Christian character. When the principle is

followed and the Lord's will is done all business relations will be just. Righteous dealing requires that
good measure be given, fair prices be required, only
helpful articles be handled, full truth about goods
be told, and a square deal be made in every transac-
tion. The Lord requires just and righteous dealings
of all people. But merely "to do" is not enough.
There is more to life. More is required.

2. THE LORD REQUIRES MERCY

"And to love mercy." Mercy is required by the
Lord as well as justice. In a true sense no man ren-
ders to his fellows all that his fellows have a right
to expect of him who does not render to them mercy.
In a very deep sense, mercy is a part of justice.
Justice toward needy people can be done only when
all the gracious and gentle charities of heart and
hand are given. The merciful person will show
kindness toward all in every contact of life. The
merciful will deal gently with all people and seek to
do and to inspire only the best. The words of such
person will be wise and his acts will be righteous, his
character and conduct will be pleasing to God and
man. One must love mercy. It must be an element
of character. It must be a part of the very make-up
of personality, so it will prompt only right desires
and attitudes toward all people. But mercy is not
enough. More than "to love mercy" is required.

3. THE LORD REQUIRES COMPANIONSHIP

"To walk humbly with thy God." The Lord will
be thy God. One must come to know him through
personal experience and constant communion and

faithful fellowship. To walk with God requires communion, based on love, and resulting in imitation. This communion must be constant and run through all the life like a golden thread through a web. God desires that his own shall live continually grasping his hand, and conscious of his overshadowing wings at all times, and conform to his will in every act of life. Only such person can walk in sweet fellowship with the Lord. Enoch walked with God and went home with him. Elijah walked with God and was rewarded in his fellowship. John walked and talked with Jesus and gave the world the true nature of his divine life. "To walk humbly with thy God" means much. Only by his help can we walk with him. In our own strength we would falter and fail.

Thus to live up to the full requirements of God means more than a first look, as the text would reveal. The requirements result from the very nature of God and our relations to him and it is only in and through Christ now that such heights can be attained and such requirements met.

THE WITNESS WITHIN THE HEART

He that believeth on the Son of God hath the witness in himself. 1 John 5:10.

The believer in the Lord Jesus Christ has the witness in his heart of the love of God, the ability of Christ to save, the reception of Christ, and of the indwelling of the Holy Spirit. This first epistle of John assures us of these facts again and again. Let us note some of these evidences.

1. THE WITNESS OF THE ATTITUDE OF GOD

"Hereby perceive we the love of God, because he laid down his life for us" (3:16). "In this was manifested the love of God toward us, because that God sent his only begotten Son into the world, that we might live through him" (4:9). These verses show the loving attitude of the Father toward lost souls. What more could he do? What more could we expect? What further assurance should we desire? This witness of his great love is in the heart of every believer in Christ.

2. THE WITNESS OF THE EFFICACY OF CHRIST TO SAVE

"God hath given to us eternal life, and this life is in his Son" (5:11). "He that hath the Son hath life" (5:12). "Whosoever believeth that Jesus is the Christ is born of God" (5:1). "This is the victory that overcometh the world, even our faith"

(5:4). Christ is able to save even to the uttermost. He saves when faith accepts. This is the assurance of the Word of God. This is the testimony of the heart that has believed. The believer has this witness in himself.

3. THE WITNESS OF RECEPTION OF CHRIST

"We know that we have passed from death unto life, because we love the brethren" (3:14). "Hereby we do know that we know him, if we keep his commandments" (2:3). The believer is assured that he has accepted Christ into his heart and life because he loves people and loves the Lord and his Word, and desires to live in accord with the will of God. This is the inner witness. This is evidence that he has been accepted by the Lord Jesus Christ.

4. THE WITNESS OF THE INDWELLING OF THE HOLY SPIRIT

Christ promised that he would send the Holy Spirit to abide with and within them for ever. "We know that he abideth in us, by the Spirit which he hath given us" (3:24). "Hereby know we that we dwell in him, and he in us, because he hath given us of his Spirit" (4:13). The believer is assured of the indwelling of the Holy Spirit by the attitude of love, mercy, kindness, and gentleness which is created in his heart. God dwells in the believer. The believer is assured of this by his Spirit.

Have faith in God. By faith accept his Son and receive eternal life and have the assurance which the Father intends you shall have. "He that believeth on the Son hath the witness in himself."

A WORKMAN OF THE LORD

Study to shew thyself approved unto God, a workman that needeth not to be ashamed, rightly dividing the word of truth. 2 Timothy 2:15.

These are the words of the aged apostle Paul to young Timothy. As he admonishes him to become a good workman of the Lord, so would he admonish all believers. Work is honorable. A good workman will be honored. Every Christian should be a good workman for the Lord. Note some of the ideas in the text.

1. THE WORKMAN OF THE LORD SHOULD BE DILIGENT

"Study." Or, as the American Standard Version puts it, "Give diligence." The Christian worker should be faithful in general and specific preparation for the particular service of the Lord committed to him. In the performance of this service for the Lord he should be faithful, devoted, honest, efficient, and energetic. The work of the Lord must be done well, for the Lord has done all things well and he deserves the best from his servants. Every deed for the Lord and his church and kingdom is worthy of the best in the workman. Be diligent.

2. THE WORKMAN OF THE LORD SHOULD BE ACCEPTABLE

"Shew thyself approved unto God." The good workman of the Lord will do all he can to meet the approval of the Lord. He will seek to please the

Lord in every thought, act, and word. Some may strive to please himself or his family or fellows, his church or community, his day or denomination, but the servant of the Lord should strive to please God even if all others are displeased. Jesus said, "I do always those things that please him" (John 8:29). The workman who pleases the Lord will eventually win the praise of the best on earth and all in heaven. Make sure that you are pleasing unto God in your life and service.

3. THE WORKMAN OF THE LORD SHOULD BE CONFIDENT

"That needeth not to be ashamed." The good workman will have faith and be courageous in service. He will have faith in God and in his purposes and plans; in himself and his ability to do what God has called him to do; in the gospel of Christ to perform with power among all people; in the church as the agency of God for advancing the kingdom; in the power of the Holy Spirit to convict of sin, righteousness, and judgment; and in the Bible as the sufficient rule and guide for faith and practice. With such faith a workman can afford to be bold in the Lord. He will not be ashamed.

4. THE WORKMAN OF THE LORD SHOULD BE CAPABLE

"Rightly dividing the word of truth." The good workman will know the eternal truth of God and what it can do, and just what is needed in each place and how to plant the truth where it can do its work. Truth must be effectively applied to meet each need of the heart. To apply the right truth in the right way at the right time to the needy heart requires divine skill. Only the Lord can lead to such efficiency, but he can and is willing to help the anxious workman. We should see that the truth of God is given to each needy heart for its highest interest.

The good workman of the Lord will be diligent, acceptable, faithful, and capable in the service of the Master.

A CALL TO WORSHIP

O worship the Lord in the beauty of holiness.
Psalm 96:9.

Here is a call for all men to wait in worship before the Lord of heaven and earth. He is worthy of worship. He deserves the devotion of all men.

1. WE SHOULD CALL ALL PEOPLE TO WORSHIP

The text is without a stated subject. It is a call to all men to worship. In fact the following verses in this psalm call on the heavens to rejoice, and the earth to be glad, and the field to be joyful, and all the trees of the woods to rejoice before the Lord. Surely if the inanimate things of earth can rejoice before the Lord, all men should worship him in deed and in truth.

2. WE SHOULD ENJOY THE PRIVILEGES OF WORSHIP

To worship God should be counted the greatest privilege of life. Men assemble themselves to see pictures, to observe great games, to hear various addresses, and to do many other things, but no privilege is greater than that of worship. In our land we have this blessed privilege which is denied so many people of other nations of the world today.

3. WE SHOULD ADORE THE PERSON OF WORSHIP

"O worship the Lord." We worship the supreme God who created the universe and sustains all. We worship God as our Father. We worship him as the

Giver and Sustainer of life. We worship God as
our Saviour and Redeemer. We adore the Lord.
We praise his holy name. To him we lift up our
hands and hearts. "O worship the Lord."

4. WE SHOULD KNOW THE PURPOSE OF WORSHIP

We worship to exalt the name of the Lord. It is
to show our love and devotion and adoration to him.
It is also that we may look unto him to become like
him in love, holiness, righteousness, justice, and
mercy. It is also that we may provoke others to
live for him and to do good works in his name. To
worship the Lord will lift a people.

5. WE SHOULD ASSEMBLE IN THE PLACE OF WORSHIP

"In the beauty of holiness" is translated in the
margin as "In the glorious sanctuary." It is possible for men to worship the Lord in the home, in the
open spaces, under a brush arbor, in a barn, or on
the highway, but we are persuaded that the most
sincere worship is in the holy house of the Lord. All
over our land there are houses of the Lord erected
and dedicated for worship. Attend the place of
worship.

Be one of the people to know the purpose of worship and enjoy its privileges in the dedicated place
for divine praise to our Lord God.

INDEX OF SCRIPTURE SELECTIONS